D0633249

GHOST TOWNS, GAMBLERS & GOLD

By CHUCK LAWLISS

GHOST TOWNS, GAMBLERS & GOLD

written and photographed by CHUCK LAWLISS

GALLERY BOOKS
An imprint of W.H. Smith Publishers Inc.
112 Madison Avenue
New York, New York 10016

Published by Gallery Books
A division of W.H. Smith Publishers, Inc.
112 Madison Avenue, New York, NY 10016
Prepared and produced by Wieser & Wieser, Inc.
118 East 25th Street
New York, NY 10010

Third Printing
Printed in Hong Kong
ISBN 0-8317-3903-7

Designed by Diane Cook

Jacket photograph by Gill Kenny/Image Bank

Contents

CALIFORNIA **10**
Sutter's Mill 12
Old Sacramento 16
Mother Lode 22
Angels Camp 24
Columbia 26
Fiddletown 30
Auburn 34
Grass Valley 38
Rough and Ready 40
Empire Mines 42
Other Mother Lode Towns 46
Death Valley 50
Bodie 60
Calico 66

ARIZONA **72**
Jerome 74
Gold King Mine 78
Tortilla Flat 82
Superstition Mountains 86
Old Tucson 88
Tombstone 96
Gleeson 104
Bisbee 108

NEW MEXICO **114**
Madrid 116
Dos Cabezas 124
White Oaks 126
Mogollon 128
Pinos Altos 132
Shakespeare 136
Lincoln 140
Fort Union 144

COLORADO **148**
Cripple Creek 150
Leadville 154
Fairplay 160
Silver Plume 164
Georgetown 166
St. Elmo 170
Telluride 174

UTAH **176**
Old Deseret Village 178
Salt Lake City 182
Heber City 184
Spring Canyon 186
Grafton 190

NEVADA **194**
Rhyolite 196
Tonopah 200
Goldfield 204
Belmont 208
Goldpoint 212
Virginia City 216
Bowers Mansion 222

Introduction

From the Rockies to the Pacific, from the border of Mexico to the Klondike, hundreds upon hundreds of ghost towns dot the American landscape, silent reminders of an age when men sought their fortunes with picks and shovels. It took the peculiar nature of mining—its boom-or-bust fickleness—to cause a town to spring up overnight, flourish, then suddenly die. I have seen abandoned communities in Hawaii, my native Vermont, and England. In those places, though, they are called deserted villages. Ghost towns are phenomena only of the American West.

In a word association game, the word "West" usually elicits the response "cowboy." But for every cowboy, there have been a hundred miners in the West. In the last half of the eighteenth century, the incredible mineral riches of the West were a far greater lure than its open ranges. The Gold Rush was one of the greatest mass migrations the world has ever known. It increased the population of California tenfold in a decade, and sent four million people to the West in forty years. The Gold Rush also changed the flow of history. Despite its remoteness, California was admitted to the Union four years before Minnesota.

Then there was the matter of the Western ethos, believed to have originated with the cowboy. According to the Western ethos, a man should be individualistic, taciturn, a loner, distrustful of government and big business, a seeker—not of security but opportunity—an existentialist. But all of these qualities fit a prospector as well as a cowboy. This is not an attempt to disparage the cowboy, but to focus some long overdue attention on the early miner, who is in danger of becoming the forgotten man of the West.

Hollywood is the villain for ignoring the miners, and focusing on the cowboys. We grew up on a diet of cowboy movies, but there have been precious few movies about Western miners.

Ghost towns, too, have been stereotyped by Hollywood. Most of us have an image of the quintessential ghost town. The setting is desolate, one street lined with false-front buildings, the wood weathered to a dark brown. Some buildings are crumbling, others stand at a crazy angle. A door is creaking in the wind, and tumbleweed rolls by.

Ghost towns that fit this description are still around, but not too many. Most ghost towns are little more than sites; the partial foundations of buildings, the detritus of abandoned mines. Others are more grandiose—with soaring pillars, arches, domes—places with an exciting past, but little present, and no future.

Finally there are towns—Virginia City, Cripple Creek, and Tombstone are examples—that live on in a fashion by making tourists believe they are something they stopped being a long time ago.

In preparing this book I visited more than a hundred ghost towns in six states: California, Nevada, Utah, Colorado, New Mexico, and Arizona—a journey of nearly twelve thousand miles. The ghost towns included in this book are simply the ones that caught my fancy—the ones that excited my imagination. A purist might well question some of my choices, but this book isn't written for purists. This book is for those who haven't as yet had the pleasure of seeing in ghost towns the reflections of a fascinating era.

Before setting out on my trip, I had thought I knew the West reasonably well. After all, I had been in most of the major cities of the West at one time or another, and I had driven across the country three times. How wrong I was! It isn't until you spend time in the small towns and talk to the people—that you can get the feel of a place. I learned that each state has a distinct look and character. Arizona and New Mexico are quite different, and neither of them resembles Nevada or California in the slightest.

If this book stimulates you to visit a few ghost towns, let me make some suggestions. First, get a local guide book to ghost towns—there is at least one for every Western state. Guide books give precise instructions on how to get there, and what the road conditions are. Many towns you'll find, can be reached only with a four-wheel drive vehicle. Second, if it's a true ghost town, bring food and water—certainly water if you're traveling in the summer. Third, watch where you step. Tumbledown buildings and junk piles are natural habitats for snakes. Finally, resist the temptation to collect souvenirs. Ghost towns are fragile things anyway, most of them well along the road to oblivion. As the saying goes, "Take only photographs, leave only footprints."

CALIFORNIA

Gold: The rush was on, the greatest migration the world has ever seen. It made some men rich, broke thousands of others, and irrevocably changed the course of history.

Sutter's Mill

Captain John Augustus Sutter, a Swiss, founded New Helvetia on a land grant from Mexico in 1839, the first outpost of civilization in inland California. He built a fort near the Sacramento River, and one of his outlying enterprises was a saw mill. It was here on January 24, 1848, that his foreman, James Marshall, saw something shining at the bottom of the mill race. "I reached my hand down and picked it up," he would recall. "It made my heart thump, for I was certain it was gold."

Marshall's discovery was ignored at first. A San Francisco newspaper gave it four lines on its back page. But Sam Brannan, who owned a general store near the mill, investigated and found gold there for the picking. He filled a bottle with nuggets and headed for San Francisco. "Gold! Gold from the American River," he shouted. This time San Francisco believed what it heard and saw. Practically all of its 450 citizens dropped what they were doing and headed for Sutter's Mill.

For the first year, the gold rush was pretty much a local phenomenon. A group came from Sonora, Mexico, and some from the Oregon Territory, but most of the miners were Californians. In the East, the first reports of the strike were discounted. The government asked the Army to investigate, however, and liked what it heard. In January 1849, President James K. Polk told Congress in his State of the Union Address, "The accounts of gold in that territory [California]

On a hill above Sutter's Mill, a statue of James Marshall (**above**) *points to where he discovered gold. Wealth and happiness were not to be his. Misfortunes left him a penniless embittered recluse. He is buried under the monument.*
At the state historical park, a full-sized replica of the mill (**right**) *stands where the original did in 1848. Early miners tore down the mill to build cabins.*

are of such an extraordinary character as would command belief." The gold rush now had the blessing of the President.

For the thousands upon thousands who headed West, there was no easy way to go. Indians, towering mountains, and 1,800 miles of desert awaited those going by land. It took six months to sail around Cape Horn to California. Some would sail to Panama, cross the isthmus on mules, and await another ship. But Panama was fever-ridden and it might be months before another ship came.

But come they did. Soon the waterfront of San Francisco was filled with rotting clipper ships; the crews had deserted and gone to the gold fields. In 1849, more than a hundred thousand people arrived to seek their fortunes.

The town of Coloma quickly grew up around the mill. There were two thousand living on the banks of the river within six months; ten thousand a year later. Coloma's Emmanual Episcopal Church (*right*) was built in 1856 and, presumably, helped curb the excesses of the miners.

Panning for gold (above) *was the technique used by early miners. Gold, being heavier than the other materials, would sink to the bottom of the swirling pan as everything else was washed away. A pan, pick, and shovel were the three essential mining tools. James Marshall made the mistake of telling the early miners that he had supernatural powers to find gold. They pestered him until he became a recluse in his cabin* (below) *near the present-day monument.*

Old Sacramento

As the link between the gold fields and the outside world, the community founded by Captain Sutter became the nucleus of California's first great city. Shortly after gold was discovered there in 1848, Sutter's Fort was laid out as a town and its name changed to Sacramento. Two years later, the first California legislature incorporated it as a city, selected it as the site of the first assembly, and, in 1854, it became the state's permanent capital.

Transportation was the key to Sacramento's importance. Ships could bypass San Francisco and sail 67 miles up the Sacramento River and load at Sacramento's docks. Sutter's Fort was the western terminus of the wagon trains of the early pioneers, and, a few years later, the Pony Express. The first transcontinental railroad, the Central Pacific—now the Southern Pacific—was begun in Sacramento in 1863 and completed six years later, an enterprise conceived and financed by four wealthy Sacramento merchants.

No state ever grew with the speed of California, and it was the Gold Rush that was the impetus. There were fewer than 25,000 Americans in California when gold was discovered in 1848. The number had quadrupled in two years. The population was 380,000 in 1860, 560,000 in 1870, and 864,000 in 1880. Sacramento and later San Francisco were the prime beneficiaries of this growth.

Men flocked to the gold fields to make their fortune, and a few did. But only a few. A much less risky road to riches was to have been a merchant selling food and supplies to the miners. Everything from picks, pans, and shovels to salt pork went for what the traffic could bear, and the traffic could bear a lot. Prices were outrageous.

A popular attraction in Sacramento is Sutter Fort (*above and opposite*). It has been accurately restored to give an informative representation of life in California just before gold was discovered.

A statue of a Pony Express rider (above) *in Old Sacramento is a reminder of the days when the West was linked to the East only by brave young men on horseback. A hardware store* (below) *was the beginning of the fortunes of two of California's Big Four—Collis Huntington and Mark Hopkins. Along with Leland Stanford and Charles Crocker, they dominated financial activities in the state for decades, and their influence is still felt today.*

Wells Fargo & Co. (**below**) *grew up in Sacramento as a stage coach company. It also hauled freight to the Mother Lode towns, and bullion back to the Sacramento banks. Railroads played an important part in the growth of Sacramento, and the development of California. The western part of the first intercontinental railroad started in Sacramento. There is an exceptional railroad museum in Old Sacramento. This display* (**above**) *is part of an early campaign train.*

The Mother Lode

As the Gold Rush progressed, miners fanned out from Coloma, finding gold, seemingly every few miles. There was one rich vein of gold, the Mother Lode, that ran from Melones in the south to Nevada City in the foothills of the Sierra Buttes in the north, a distance of some 270 miles. Along the Mother Lode, mining camps sprang up, growing into towns if the gold held out, abandoned if it didn't.

In the first ten years of mining, the Mother Lode yielded up $600 million in gold. At the peak around 1860, there were some 120,000 miners in the Mother Lode country, but by 1873 the number had shrunk to 30,000. The game had changed: big companies were tunneling hundreds of feet underground, and a large number of the individual miners left were Chinese, tediously reworking the leftover gravel. Many of the miners had come down from the hills and become farmers.

Stagecoach lines* (above) *linked the towns and mining camps.
The American River* (right) *crosses the Mother Lode near Coloma.

SERBIAN ORTHODOX
CHURCH
930

Angels Camp

Two American writers took their first step toward immortality when they wrote about this wild-and-wooly mining camp. Bret Hart struck literary gold with *Luck of Roaring Camp*, Mark Twain with *The Celebrated Jumping Frog of Calaveras County*. Both were classic short stories that captured the imagination.

Bret Harte came to California in 1854 to join his mother who had married a San Francisco man after his father died. Harte went to the mines in 1855, taught school for awhile, and did a bit of mining. Mining camp life didn't appeal to the effete Harte. He confided that he found the Mother Lode country "hard, ugly, unwashed, vulgar, and lawless." Back in San Francisco, he became a successful newspaperman, magazine editor, and writer. His distaste for the camps notwithstanding, Harte mined this literary lode for the rest of his life.

Mark Twain was 26-years-old and still known as Sam Clemens when he accompanied his brother west in 1861. He tried prospecting in Nevada and California with no success, worked on the *Enterprise* in Virginia City (where he first used the pseudonym Mark Twain) before moving to San Francisco in 1864. There he met Harte, who helped him find a publisher for his stories. Later that year, Mark Twain went to Angels Camp and stayed with a family that were friends of Harte. At the Angels Hotel he heard the story of the jumping frog. By the time he left California the following year, he had collected material about mines and miners that he used the rest of his life. Unlike Harte, Mark Twain liked the miner's life. "I know the mines and miners interiorly as well as Bret Harte knows them exteriorly," he once wrote.

Bret Harte was a master at creating character and mood in a few well-shaped sentences, but the American West had found its voice in the vitality and exuberance of Mark Twain.

A larger-than-life statue of Mark Twain* (above) *stands in a park at Angels Camp, the setting for his famous* The Celebrated Jumping Frog of Calaveras County. *The ore-filled mine car next to the church* (opposite) *graphically illustrates the occupation of its early parishoners.

Columbia

In March 1850, Dr. Thaddeus Hildreth, his brother, and some other prospectors camped on a rainy night in the area that was to become Columbia. In the morning, they decided to try their luck panning for gold. Before they were through, they had found thirty pounds of gold. The area was a geological oddity: a limestone bed full of holes had captured and retained the gold that had washed down from the hills over millions of years. Before the month had passed, some five thousand miners were living in a tent town called Hildreth's Diggins.

The town almost died when the runoff water from the spring thaws dried up, and there was no way to work the dirt. Soon there were only a handful of miners left, hauling the dirt to water some miles away. The Tuolumne Water Company was formed, and by the following April a complicated system of ditches and reservoirs was bringing enough water to the site for full-scale mining.

The town, renamed Columbia, quickly grew to a city of 20,000—a population practically as large as San Francisco's at that time. Two disastrous fires destroyed most of the early frame structures and were replaced by brick buildings. When sluicing (the use of high-powered hoses to wash away the limestone and extract the gold) was introduced, the brick buildings were torn down to get at the gold-bearing limestone beneath them. Sluicing did such severe ecological damage that it was soon banned by the state.

Columbia's boom days were to last 20 years—and what years they were! Edwin Booth played Richard III to an audience of miners at the Fallon House theater, followed a few weeks later by Lola Montez performing her Spider Dance. There was an arena built for fights between bulls and bears. Horace Greeley, editor of the *New York Tribune*, wrote about the fights, likening the contestants to speculators on Wall Street, terms which quickly found their way into the language.

The stucco has worn off the brick at the Columbia Jail* (above)*, but it still looks sturdy enough to keep prisoners from wandering.
There's a lot for a visitor to do in Columbia: take a ride on the stagecoach* (opposite)*, pan for gold in a nearby stream, watch a blacksmith at work, or relax and sip sarsaparilla.

ENGINE COMPANY

*The fire house (***opposite***) has an elaborately decorated hand pumper, made for the King of Hawaii, that was stranded in San Francisco when the ship's crew deserted and went to the gold fields. Visitors can try their hand at panning gold (***above***), or just roam the streets and enjoy such sights as this old miner's wagon (***below***).*

Fiddletown

Winter was approaching, but the miners, most of them fresh from Missouri, were too busy panning gold along the Consumnes River to notice. Only when the snow started to fall did they think about shelter more substantial than their tents. The winter was long and wet, and the cooped-up miners spent their time playing on their fiddles such old favorites as "Turkey in the Straw." When it came time to name their town, Fiddletown seemed the logical choice.

Fiddletown prospered through the years. It had four hotels, a brewery, and a winery. Like most mining camps, Fiddletown had a Chinatown with its own stores, medicine shops, joss houses and opium dens.

Two colorful judges presided in Fiddletown. Judge Yates is remembered for an incident in one of his trials. A witness was playing fast and loose with the truth when the judge banged his gavel and shouted, "This court is adjourned!" After a dramatic pause, the judge yelled, "This man is a damn liar!" Another pause and he reconvened the court.

Judge Purinton found that when he visited San Francisco and Sacramento,people made sport of him when they discovered he came from a place named Fiddletown. Without consulting his fellow townsmen, the judge had the town's name changed to Oleta. A year or so later, when the judge had calmed down, the town changed its name back to Fiddletown.

Fiddletown is a bit off the tourist trail, and is quiet most of the year. In the summer, though, it is host to a fiddlin' contest and thousands of participants and lovers of country music crowd its main street.

One of the few surviving buildings in Fiddletown (*above*) is a bit worse for wear. At one time, Fiddletown had the largest Chinatown outside of San Francisco, in California.
***The general store (*opposite*) has been catering to the needs of Fiddletown for more than 130 years. Fiddletown was the setting for one of Bret Harte's stories of Gold Rush days,* "An Episode in Fiddletown."**

FIDDLETOWN
STORE
U.S. POST O
LETOWN,

BUTTE STORE

There are buildings of historic interest throughout the Mother Lode. Two of particular interest are shown here. The International Order of Odd Fellows building (**above*****) is one of the oldest in Mokelumne Hill. The Ginocchio store (*****opposite*****) is all that's left of the once bustling town of Butte City. The store was built in 1856 and now is protected as a landmark.***

Auburn

On his way to Sutter's Mill, Claude Chana, a friend of James Marshall, stopped at a ravine to try his luck panning for gold. The first pan yielded up three excellent nuggets, and in less than a week a mining camp had sprung up. It was known by several names, before some nostalgic New Yorkers decided to name it after their hometown—Auburn.

The surface gold was soon exhausted, but an accident kept the boom going. A miner had dug a ditch to carry water to his claim. The flow suddenly stopped and he found that the water was pouring into a gopher hole. The bottom of the hole was covered with gold, $40,000 worth, as it turned out. A switch to hydraulic mining kept the Auburn mines productive for another decade.

A second town developed above the ravine. This was fortunate, because a fire in 1855 took just 25 minutes to destroy the old town. It also was a transportation center; trails led from mining camps in the Sierra, and in 1865 the Central Pacific was routed through town. Auburn had too much going for it to become a ghost town.

Auburn leaves nothing to the imagination in marking the location where its hanging tree once stood (*above*).
Two 1857 Victorians (*opposite*) were used as lawyers' offices. The streets in Auburn once were paths to the diggings, and angle off in every direction.

CHAMBER COMMERCE
ASSAY
30
ORNAMENTS
DECORATIONS

After the disastrous fire in Auburn, the town was rebuilt in brick, producing some priceless examples of Victorian architecture

J.S.
1861
12 MIN ZONE

Grass Valley

Grass Valley emerged from the early Gold Rush days as the most important gold-mining town in the state, primarily because it was here that hard-rock mining techniques were introduced and developed. At Grass Valley, mining changed from a hit-or-miss business of individual miners into an industry.

For this reason, there was no boom-and-bust-cycle here. Grass Valley grew throughout the last half of the nineteenth century as the Empire, the North Star, and other mines in the area prospered. In the process, it became the commercial and social center of the Northern Mines. But for anyone with romance in his soul, Grass Valley was, first and foremost, the home of Lola Montez and Lotta Crabtree.

Born Eliza Gilbert in Ireland, Lola Montez charmed Europe with her singing and dancing, and scandalized Europe with her two year affair with Ludwig of Bavaria. She was famous for her parties: Alexander Dumas, Franz Liszt, and Victor Hugo were among her frequent guests. On an 1852 American tour, she was not well received in California and decided to retire to Grass Valley. It was to be an active retirement: she kept monkeys and a grizzly bear for pets, and resumed giving her famous parties.

One day Lola met and was enchanted by Lotta Crabtree, a seven-year-old girl who lived nearby. Lola took Lotta as a protégée, teaching her songs and dances. The Crabtrees moved away the next year, but Lola had done her job well. Lotta started performing in a saloon at age eight, and the miners showered her with nuggets. She toured the camps for years, became a success in San Francisco, New York, and the Continent. Lotta Crabtree retired at a comparatively young age and continued to live well. When she died in 1924, she left a $4 million estate.

Lola Montez did not fare as well. An Australian tour in 1855 was a flop. She returned to America and tried the lecture circuit, but failed again. She died nearly penniless in 1861 at the age of 43.

Small, but exquisite, Emmanual Church (above) is one of the architectural treasures of Grass Valley.
The view from the front door of Lola Montez's house (opposite).
Up this walk one day in 1853 came seven-year-old Lotta to meet Lola—a happenstance that was to lead to a brilliant career for Lotta on the stage.

Rough and Ready

Most of the miners who settled here had served in the Mexican War under General Zachary "Rough and Ready" Taylor, so they named the town after him. It was founded in 1849 and thrived for 20 years, but its moment of fame came in 1850.

The United States had passed a miner's tax, and the Territory of California had announced its intention to collect it. When news of this reached Rough and Ready, it seemed just the sort of thing that had cramped the miners' lives back East. After some heated discussion they voted to secede from the territory and the United States, and form the "Great Republic of Rough and Ready." But how could the Great Republic of Rough and Ready celebrate the Fourth of July if it was a separate country? The miners voted themselves back into the Union.

The grange* (above) *is one of the few remaining buildings in this town which once seceded from the union. A nearby barn* (right) *takes on a festive air as the Fourth of July approaches.

The Empire Mine

The story goes that a miner named George Knight was out looking for his cow one moonlight night when he stubbed his toe, knocking loose a rock near the Boston Ravine. Particles in the rock glittered, so George took it to be assayed and found that it was gold-bearing quartz, the first to be found in the Mother Lode country. Within a few years, hundreds of miles of tunnels were dug around Grass Valley and Nevada City; the era of hard-rock gold mining in California had begun.

If prospectors working independently in a boom-or-bust atmosphere was the rule in the mining camps, the Empire Mine was one of a few notable exceptions. The Empire, the oldest, largest, and richest gold mine in California, operated continuously from 1850 to 1956 and probably wouldn't have closed then if the price of gold hadn't seemed permanently fixed at $32 an ounce. The Empire employed as many as 800 miners at a time who worked in shifts and, who, over the years, dug 5.8 million ounces of gold out of the mine's 367 miles of tunnels.

In the early days, Cornish miners were brought from England to help develop hard-rock mining techniques suitable to California and to train inexperienced miners. Miners were lowered into the mine on cars; one descent covered a 4,000-foot decline in four minutes. In the

*Near the office of the Empire Mine is a weathered relic (***above***) of the days when gold was $32 an ounce and gas was 32 cents a gallon.*
*Gold-bearing quartz was fed from this shed (***opposite***) to the stamping machines that crushed it in a continuous roar that made conversation impossible anywhere near the mine. Old-time residents of Nevada City claimed they could predict the weather by changes in the sound of the roar from the mine.*

The home of William Bourn, the Empire's owner, (**opposite*****) was called the Bourn Cottage, but mansion might have been a more descriptive word. Mr. Bourn also had an estate in Woodside, California, and didn't spend more time than necessary at the noisy mine. A formal English rose garden adjoins the Bourn Cottage. Nearby is the handsome Empire Clubhouse, which was used to house and entertain guests of the mine. The tree-shaded, manicured area shared by the cottage and the clubhouse are in sharp contrast to the look of no-nonsense efficiency of the mine.***

tunnels, quartz was dug out of the vein with picks and shovels and, later, jack hammers, and brought to the surface in mine cars where it was pulverized by 84 huge stamping machines, each with 1,750-pound stamps that slammed down 104 times a minute—an ear-splitting racket that could be heard miles away.

The pulverized ore then was passed over amalgamation plates that trapped the gold with mercury. The mercury was removed by retorting, the gold was then melted and cast into bars. A later refinement increased the amount of gold taken from the quartz to 90 percent by using cyanide to recover more gold from the residue of the amalgamation.

The Empire Mine now is a state historical park, and a visit there is an excellent introduction to hard-rock gold mining in all its size and complexity, and a reminder of the wealth it produced. There is a small museum and a 2-mile trail through the mine's 784 acres.

Miners were lowered to work down this incline (**above*****) on a car with rows of bleacherlike seats. Each mine developed its own system of bell signals to warn miners of possible dangers. Working at levels that reached more than 3,000 feet in depth, miners risked cave-ins, fires and floods, should the huge pumps that drained the tunnels cease to function.***

BELL SIGNALS

1	Bell	Hoist
2	"	Lower
1	"	Stop if in Motion
3-1	"	Hoist Men
3-2	"	Lower Men
2-1	"	Release Skip or Truck
7	"	Accident, move truck or skip on Verbal Orders only
7	"	Followed by station Signal Send truck with Stretcher and Help to Station indicated

Signal for This Station — Bells or Flashes

RULES

IF - after giving a Signal you get a flash from the Engineer, it means either that you gave the wrong signal, or that the signal was not clear to the Engineer. Repeat the Signal.

IF - either bell line is out of order, use other line, ringing 2 bells just before signal to Hoist or Lower, as 3-2-1 Bells, Hoist Man.

To call Truck, or Skip use Telephone. Tell Engineer where you are and where you want to go.

Riding on Bail of Skip absolutely prohibited.

Do not get on or off while truck or skip is in motion.

Keep hands down while riding.

[illegible]

[illegible]

Mother Lode Towns

In addition to the Mother Lode towns featured in these pages, there are others of particular interest, both historically and aesthetically. They are listed here geographically, south to north.

Hornitos

Mexican miners founded this town after they were forced to leave nearby Quartzburg. The legendary bandit Joaquin Murieta is said to have made Hornitos his headquarters. Murieta swore vengeance against his American prosecutors after they beat him, raped his wife, and murdered his brother. He was a Robin Hood of the Southern Mines in the 1850's. Many historical markers mention his name, but fact and fiction have been hopelessly entwined.

Chinese Camp

In the early 1850' some five thousand Chinese miners settled here, and a minor incident at the mines was later to ignite a tong war. A large stone happened to roll from the diggings of one group of miners, to a spot where another group was working, and a fight started. Each group was allied to a San Francisco tong, and each sent for reinforcements. On Octobe 25, 1856, 1,200 members of one tong faced 900 of th other. All were armed, and in the melee four wer killed and twelve injured. American law authoritie took 250 into custody. Honor had been upheld an everyone returned to the mines satisfied.

Sonora

Bad blood between Mexican and American miners marked the early days of Sonora. A state-wide, $20-a-month tax was levied on all foreign miners. The Mexicans left, cutting Sonora's five thousand population almost in half. Business suffered until the tax was repealed and the foreign miners returned. Sonora was the richest of the Southern Mine towns. In the 1870's, three partners bought a supposedly played out pocket mine from a group of Chileans. Long digging brought the new owners to a vein of almost solid gold. Within a week, more than $500,000 in gold was mined and shipped.

Placerville

Three great American fortunes trace their beginnings to this early mining camp. From 1853 to 1858, J. M. Studebaker built wheelbarrows in his Main Street shop. When he had saved $8,000, he went home to South Bend, Indiana, and with his brothers built the largest covered wagon factory in the country. Two of his Placerville tradesmen were Philip Armour, a butcher, and grocer Mark Hopkins. Placerville was first known as Dry Diggin's because water was in such short supply. In 1849, the name was changed to Hangtown after a series of hangings, then became Placerville in 1854. After the mines were exhausted, the town became an important stage stop, and commercial center for the Northern Mines.

Yankee Jims

Yankee Jim wasn't a Yankee at all—but an Australian, and a horse thief. He pretended to be a miner, but concentrated on stealing horses. He kept the horses he had stolen in a corral on a high mountain ridge. One of his victims discovered his horse in Yankee Jim's corral and went for the law. Yankee Jim escaped, and in a bit of poetic justice, the corral was found to be on a small fortune in free gold. Named after the departed horse thief, Yankee Jims grew into Placer County's largest mining camp.

Nevada City

Nevada City was one of the first of the Gold Rush mining towns and still is one of the most charming. It abounds in quality Victorian buildings of historic interest. At Ott's Assay Office, for example, James Ott assayed the first samples of what was to be the Comstock Lode at Virginia City. Nevada City also was the first Gold Rush town to see Madame Eleanor Dumont, known later as Madame Moustache, the lady gambler. She stepped off the stage here in 1854, a comely young lady with good manners, and proceeded to open a blackjack parlor. When the mines started to fade four years later, she started to move around the camps. Her beauty was beginning to fade, and she had acquired a line of dark fuzz on her upper lip that give her the cruel nickname. In Bodie, twenty-five years after she first arrived in Nevada City, she committed suicide.

Altaville

For a town that had so many names, there isn't much left to look at. Altaville—previously called Forks in the Road, Winterton, and Cherokee Flat—is primarily remembered as the scene of a hoax. A skull was found in the area and was presented as that of a prehistoric man. For years, the scientific community debated its authenticity. Finally, it was determined to be the skull of a contemporary Indian, and the whole affair had been an elaborate practical joke. Bret Harte immortalized the incident in his poem, *To the Pliocene Skull*.

Mokelumne Hill

Violence was commonplace in Mok Hill, as this town was popularly known. Five people were killed in one week, and once for a seventeen week stretch, there was at least one murder every weekend. Mok Hill also had the distinction of having two foreign wars. The first was with a Dr. Concha of Chili Gulch. The doctor, a Chilean, was using countrymen as slave labor in his mines, and had registered illegal claims under the names of some of his peons. The men of Mok Hill ran Dr. Concha out of town. A few years later was the French War. French miners were successfully working a claim in the nearby hills, and made the mistake of flying a French flag over their diggings. That—and greed—were sufficient pretexts for the Mok Hill miners to drive out the French and claim the mines as their own.

Volcano

There never was a volcano here, but a natural cup in the mountains gave the town its name. Mexican War veterans from the 8th New York Regiment struck gold here in 1848, and a town quickly grew up around the diggings. The area was to produce $90 million in gold before the boom was over. Still on display in Volcano is "Old Abe," a cannon that played a role in the Civil War. When Southern sympathizers threatened to divert gold to the Confederate cause, Union volunteers wheeled out "Old Abe." There were no cannon balls in town, but they had a supply of round river stones. The Southern sympathizers gave up before a shot was fired. Volcano had the first public library in the state, the first astronomical observatory, and the first debating society.

Murphys

John and Daniel Murphy settled the area in July 1848, and the town grew into one of the most charming on the Mother Lode. Murphys Hotel, built in 1855, welcomed such guests as Ulysses S. Grant, J. Pierpont Morgan and Thomas Lipton. About twenty miles north is the Calaveras Big Trees State Park, a magnificent stand of Sequoias.

Jackass Hill

The braying of the hundreds of mules tied up at this location gave this mining camp its unusual name. Mark Twain lived in a cabin here for five months, writing, among other stories, *The Celebrated Jumping Frog of Calaveras County.* The Twain cabin is a popular visitor attraction.

Drytown

Temperance had nothing to do with naming this town. It just happened to be on Dry Creek. Founded in 1848, Drytown had a good nine-year boom before a fire leveled it. Some of the original brick buildings have survived. Nearby is the site of Lower Rancheria, a Mexican and Chilean mining camp, the scene of a massacre in 1855 by a gang of Mexican bandits. A monument marks the mass grave of twelve killed in the massacre.

North Bloomfield

A hard-drinking, garrulous old prospector who used to talk miners into coming here with his tall tales, gave the town its first name—Humbug. The town has been restored and now is part of the Malakoff Diggins State Park. A number of buildings are open to visitors: the general store, post office, blacksmith, and the fire station. At the state park are examples of what the huge hoses once used for hydraulic mining can do to the environment. Hydraulic mining caused erosion, flooding, and killed the fish in the streams. Such mining was banned by the state, but not until a lot of damage was done. Ironically, the area today is strangely beautiful.

Death Valley

A party of '49ers made the mistake of trying to reach the gold fields by crossing the alkali flats of this valley in the blazing heat of summer. Their fate gave this forbidding, but beautiful place its most appropriate name.

In prosaic terms, Death Valley is a deep trough, some 140 miles long, and from 4 to 16 miles wide. High mountains, some over 11,000 feet in elevation, rise on either side. Eons ago this was an inland sea. Violent eruptions heaved up mountain ranges, and the sun evaporated the water: 550 of the valley's 3,000 square miles are below sea level. The average annual rainfall is less than two inches. All these factors combine to make Death Valley a giant convection oven—one of the hottest places on the face of the earth. Summer temperatures of 125 degrees in the shade are common; the Western Hemisphere record of 134 degrees was set here in 1913.

There is not much life in Death Valley: coyotes, rats, and reptiles; some mesquite, desert holly, and creosote bushes.

How can a place so barren, so lifeless, be beautiful? It's the color and the sweep of the valley and the mountains, both intensified by the clarity of the dry, crystal-clear air. The mountains, high and bare, are as subtly tinted as a Japanese watercolor. There are rugged canyons that display colors from deep purple to rich gold.

The colors come from the minerals that through the millenia have drained down from the mountains—borax, nitrate of soda, copper, iron, lead, silver, and gold. Borax was discovered here in 1873, and large-scale borax mining was underway a few years later. Prospectors also discovered the copper, lead, silver, and gold in the mountains. Mining towns sprang up with such colorful names as Greenwater, Skidoo, and Crackerjack. For more than half a century, miners endured the hardships of Death Valley until the mines played out.

*A lizard (*above*) is one of the few natural inhabitants of Death Valley. The Indians had another name for the vast, treeless, alkali plains:* **Tomesha**—*ground afire.*

*The colors of Death Valley can be seen in this view of the Armargosa Range, near Furnace Creek (*opposite*). In the northern part of the valley is Ubehebe Crater, an extinct small volcano.*

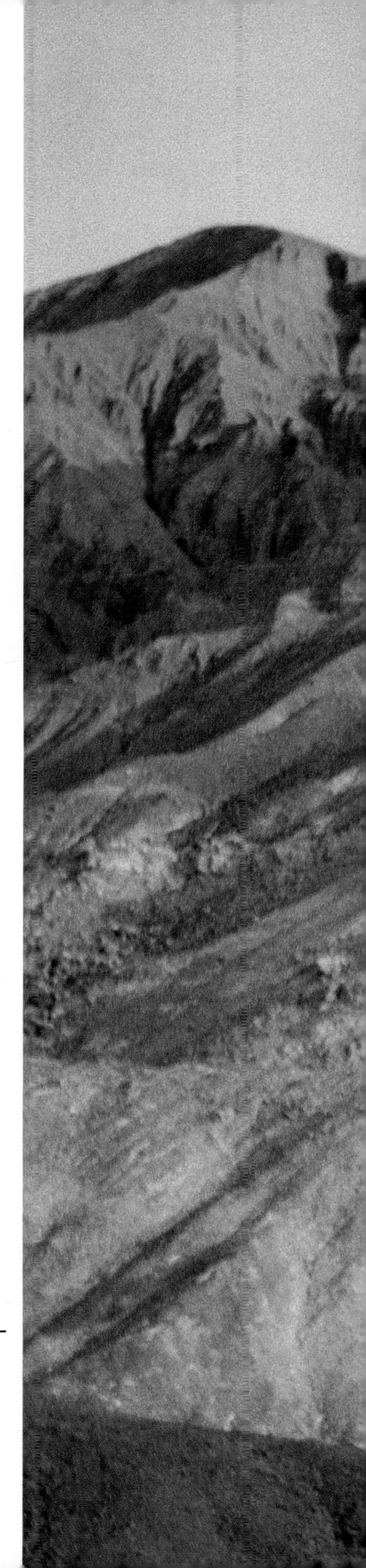

Harmony Borax Mines

From this processing plant in the badlands, near Zabriskie Point in the 1880's, the first 20-mule teams set out to carry borax to the rail head at Mojave—165 desert miles away. Two men made the trip, the driver and a swamper who looked after the mules and did the cooking. The team pulled 20,000 pounds of borax in two wagons, and 10,000 pounds of water in the water cart. The round trip took about three weeks, and one wagon load filled half a box car.

William T. Coleman built the mill here in 1882. There were several adobe and stone buildings, a warehouse, stables and offices. Crews of Chinese gathered the borax cottonballs and loaded them into one-horse carts. At the mill, the balls were put in tanks filled with water pumped from a nearby spring, carbonated soda was added, and the mixture was brought to a boil. The solution was drawn off and placed in covered tanks where rods were suspended. As the solution cooled, the refined borax crystallized on the rods.

When the temperature rose above 115 degrees, the Harmony works shut down, not for humane reasons, but because the high heat disturbed the refining process. The discovery of borax much closer to the Mojave rail head and the introduction of foreign imports forced the Harmony Works to close for good in 1888, although sporadic borax mining has been carried out in Death Valley over the years.

Adobe walls, a vat, and chimney* (above) *have survived from the 1880's, when the Harmony Borax Works was the most remote industrial mill in the country. The wagons pulled by the teams of 20 mules* (opposite) *wait in the desert as if ready to go again. The wagons are huge—the rear wheels taller than the average man.

*The entrance to the mine (***above left***) is about all that's left at Leadfield. Gold was found in 1914 at the Ashford Mines and process for shipment in the mill (***left below***). These beehive structures (***above***) were charcoal kilns. Little remains today of the once prosperous Ashford Mines (***right***).*

Scotty's Castle

In the hills near the north end of Death Valley stands Scotty's Castle, a monument to a most unusual man—Walter "Death Valley" Scot. Born in Kentucky, he headed West at an early age. He was a wrangler in Wells, Nevada, in the early 1880's, then helped drive cattle to Southern California. He later was a swamper on 20-mule teams at the Harmony Borax Mines. He left to become a trick rider for twelve years with Buffalo Bill's Wild West Show.

Scotty moved back to Death Valley in 1902, and became famous as a prospector and the owner of a gold mine. The mine probably was a figment of Scotty's imagination. What he did have was the friendship and financial backing of A. M. Johnson, a Chicago insurance executive. Johnson, as shy and retiring as Scotty was ebullient, apparently got a vicarious thrill out of making Scotty's dreams and schemes come true.

In 1905, for example, they chartered a train, renamed it the *Coyote Special*, and raced from Los Angeles to Chicago in 44 hours and 54 minutes, a record that stood until the mid-1930's. Their crowning achievement, though, was the castle. It was under construction from 1922 to 1931, and cost $1.5 million, according to the contractor.

Early prospectors found gold in these mountains south of Scotty's Castle* (above)*, but Scotty's mine was good-humored fiction, not fact.
An improbable castle in an improbable location* (opposite) *now is a major tourist attraction in Death Valley.

Here at Badwater in Death Valley is the lowest point in the Western Hemisphere—282 feet below sea level. The whiteness of the alkali flats and the clarity of the dry air give Badwater a surrealistic quality. Visitors walking across the flats seem as other-worldly as characters in a Fellini film.

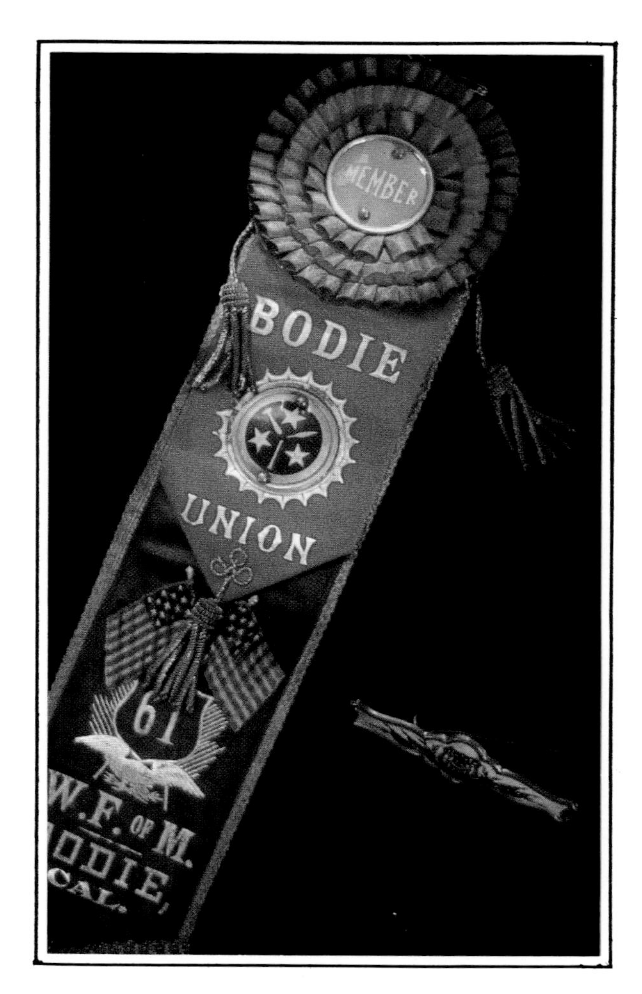

Bodie

One of the legends of the West concerns the "Bad Man from Bodie." Whether the "bad man" was a real person or not, Bodie did have a reputation of being the roughest, toughest mining camp anywhere. With a population of 10,000 at its zenith, Bodie averaged roughly one killing a day. The tide of violence prompted the *Bodie Standard* to editorialize: "There is some irresistible power that impels us to cut and shoot each other to pieces." Another newspaper reported that a young girl, upon learning that her family was moving to Bodie, concluded her prayers with, "Good-bye, God, I'm going to Bodie."

In 1865, *Harper's Monthly* sent writer I. Ross Browne to investigate the town's reputation for wickedness. His story confirmed that there indeed was a flagrant disregard of law and order. This report didn't upset the citizens of Bodie. To the contrary, they named their main street after Mr. Browne.

Two of Bodie's bad men waylaid the stage from Bodie to Carson City and relieved it of $30,000 in gold bullion. They were caught a few hours later, one bandit was killed, and the other wounded in the capture. But the gold was missing. The second bandit died in jail that night. More than a century later, the gold has yet to be recovered.

Miners were intensely loyal to their union, (**above*****) for it helped them earn $5 a day in an age when the average laborer was lucky to get a quarter of that. Everything was expensive in towns like Bodie, though, and this negated much of the miners' economic advantage.***
Bodie today is far and away the most extensive and best preserved ghost town in the West. There are nearly a hundred wood buildings still standing. Years of weathering have turned them a rich dark brown (**opposite*****).***

GOLD

A store in town (**opposite below**) *still displays its vintage wares. Bodie now is a state park and many of the houses are furnished. The feeling in Bodie is of the past preserved, not restored or recreated.*
The Bodie firehouse was located near the mines (**opposite above**) *for good reason—the mines were lit by open candles and if a fire broke out it could quickly exhaust the oxygen in the tunnels, suffocating the men below.*
The passing of the years has left this house erect, but listing a bit to starboard (**right**).
At sunset (**overleaf**) *Bodie has a strange beauty.*

There were 65 saloons in Bodie. On the outskirts of town were two cemeteries, one for "decent, respectable folks," and another, far larger one, for all the rest. One preacher termed Bodie a "sea of sin, lashed by the tempests of lust and passion." In June 1881, the *Bodie Daily Free Press* commented, "Bodie is becoming a quiet summer resort—no one killed here last week."

Perhaps the weather wasn't conducive to law and order. In the winter, temperatures of 20 and 30 degrees below zero were common, the wind blowing snow into 10 to 20-foot drifts. Despite its notoriety, Bodie produced $75 million in gold over the years.

Bodie is set on a barren, rolling hilltop in a remote part of the state near the Nevada border. There are no food or overnight facilities, and it's a 13-mile drive on a rough, washboard road from the highway, so a visitor usually has the town pretty much to himself. The altitude is 7,500 feet, and with the wind usually blowing, it is chilly, even in the summer. To walk the streets is to feel an acute sense of loneliness and desolation. One thinks, "If there are truly ghosts, there are ghosts in Bodie."

Calico

Walter Knott worked in the silver mines in Calico as a young man, but his fortune came, not from silver, but from what he later created near Los Angeles—Knott's Berry Farm. In 1950, the remains of Calico, which had been a ghost town since 1929, and the nearby mining claims were purchased by the Knott family. The town was lovingly restored to recreate its former glory.

Calico got its name from the Calico Mountains that surround it; they are as colorful as calico cloth. In 1881, two prospectors found silver at what was to become the Silver King Mine, the richest silver strike in California history. In the 1880's, $86 million in silver ore and $9 million in borax were mined. Veins of silver 4 feet wide were uncovered, assaying 200 to 400 ounces per ton. Many times at the Silver King, great chunks of almost pure silver were cut out of solid rock, each weighing more than half a ton. It was all hard-rock mining, and there are more than 30 miles of tunnels and shafts under and around Calico. Many of the early miners were emigrées from Cornwall, England. This was the case in many early mining camps, for Cornishmen have the reputation of being the best hard-rock miners in the world.

Calico had one street lined with adobe buildings. Many miners, though, lived in caves dug out of the canyon sides. This had one distinct advantage; caves were much cooler in the summer when temperatures in the Mojave Desert often reached 110 degrees.

In the 1880's, Calico had 22 saloons, 3 restaurants, many stores, hotels, and boarding houses, an assay office, and a school. During its heyday, the town twice was partially destroyed by fire and quickly rebuilt. The beginning of the end came for Calico in 1896, when the

An old water wagon (*above*) proudly announces that this is indeed Calico, the Mojave ghost town restored and recreated by the Knott family. The old schoolhouse (*opposite*) taught the "three R's" to the miners' children a century ago.

The Maggie Mine (above) *yielded up $86 million worth of silver before playing out. A young Japanese couple* (right) *pose as a well-dressed couple of the Gay 90's as part of their day of fun in Calico.*

An old supply wagon (above) is somewhat the worse for wear, but the diminutive steam engine (below) still can propel carloads of tourists on a short tour of the town.

price of silver fell from $1.31 to $.63 an ounce, and most of the miners moved on to more lucrative diggings.

Calico now is a San Bernardino County regional park and is the major tourist attraction in the area. It is roughly halfway between Los Angeles and Las Vegas, just off the main highway, 10 miles north of Barstow. There is a tram that takes visitors up to the town from the parking area. Other attractions include a tour of the Maggie Mine, a ride on the Calico-Odessa Railroad, a museum, a shooting gallery, a mystery shack, the Calikage Playhouse, and numerous shops and restaurants. There are special events in Calico throughout the year: a Pitchin', Cookin', and Spittin' Hullabaloo on Palm Sunday (at the 1980 Hullabaloo, one Randy Ober of Bentville, Arkansas, set the world's record by spittin' tobacco juice 44 feet 6 inches); a Barbershop, Bluegrass, and Country Music Festival on Mother's Day; and Calico Days on Columbus Day weekend, with horse parades, a burro run, and the National Gunfight Stunt Championships. It's all a far cry from the serious and dangerous business of hard-rock mining, but everyone seems to thoroughly enjoy themselves, partaking of the real and the hokum with equal gusto.

A woman had to be made of stern stuff to make a life as a wife and mother in an early mining camp. The trip to California, by land or sea, was, at best, an ordeal—months long and full of hardships, deprivations, boredom, and sometimes danger. When they arrived at the camp, they usually had to live in a tent until a crude house could be built. There was no plumbing; water had to be carried to the house, and the toilet was an outhouse. Fresh meat and vegetables were in short supply, and the desert ruled out gardens. Recreational or cultural activities had to be improvised. One woman wrote to her sister, "Really, everybody ought to go to the mines, just to see how little it takes to make people comfortable in the world."

Children presented special problems. Mines were filled with danger: deep, unguarded holes and abandoned shafts. Wild animals and snakes were commonplace. Mothers didn't like to let their children out of their sight. Rare was the camp that had a resident doctor, or a schoolteacher, for that matter. The lure of striking it rich in the mines led many men away from their professions.

All this hardship on one side of the scale was more than balanced by the pioneer spirit, the sense of building a new, better life together in a new part of the country where the future looked rosy and cloudless.

A steam-driven LaFrance fire pumper* (above) *was horse-drawn and it got its water from a hose dropped down a well or into the river. Pumpers like this replaced the bucket brigades and hand-operated pumps that were in use until about 1875. A volunteer at Calico* (opposite)*, dressed in the costume of an early settler, demonstrates one of the skills that pioneer women brought with them from the East—quilting. A bonnet provided sensible protection from the blistering desert sun.

ARIZONA

Coronado came in the 1540's for cities of gold. In the 1600's, Spaniards later forced Indians to mine for silver. But mining didn't become important here until the late nineteenth century, and the real treasure then was copper.

Jerome

The Indians used the colorful ores found in Jerome to make dyes and war paint as early as 975 A.D. In 1872, an Indian scout found evidence of this early digging. In 1876, a party of prospectors arrived in Prescott and heard the stories about Mingus Mountain, took a look, but were unimpressed. Later that year, two ranchers took out claims, but quickly sold them to the Territorial Governor for $2,000. Still nothing happened, until the Governor met a New York lawyer who was willing to finance the operation. The lawyer was Eugene Jerome, Winston Churchill's American grandfather, and he stipulated that the town be named after him.

More delays in mining occurred until 1893, when the United Verde Copper Company was incorporated and a smelter was built. A slow beginning for an area that was to produce $500 million in copper, and enough gold and silver to pay the cost of refining.

Jerome was the scene of labor troubles. In 1907, the miners won a strike that cut their day from ten to eight hours, and raised their pay to $2.75 a day. A second strike in 1917 was broken when armed company men forced several hundred miners and agitators into boxcars at gunpoint, had them taken to the middle of the desert, and dropped off.

Jerome had a population of 15,000 in 1929, including a work force of about 2,500. Production trailed off after that year and the mine was closed for good in 1953. It was the end of Jerome as a city. Population now is fewer than 500.

The mine shaft at Jerome* (above) *still towers over the town.
***As sundown approaches, Jerome seems basked in lost glory* (opposite).**

JEROME
HISTORICAL SOCIETY
GIFT SHO
JEROME HISTORICAL SOCIETY
MINE MUSEUM

A suggestion of the wealth produced by Jerome's copper mountain can be found in some of its architectural details (above). The emblem (below) graced a movie theater. Like many other Jerome buildings, it is slowly slipping down the mountain.

The mountain towers over Jerome* (above). *There are 65 miles of tunnels under Jerome, and it sits atop the Verde Fault, causing the movement of the buildings. An old Coca-Cola sign* (below) *is about to lose its battle with the elements.

Gold King Mine

A few miles from Jerome, Don and Terry Robertson, transplants from the Midwest, have purchased the Gold King and made it into a living museum of the early days of mining in Arizona.

Besides restoring the mine itself and some tumbledown buildings, Don Robertson has assembled an extensive collection of antique gas engines and restored them to working order. He takes great pleasure in firing them up, demonstrating how they work, and explaining what they were used for. The strange relics and fragments of machinery seen in other ghost towns suddenly are seen in their proper context at the Gold King.

The Gold King Mine is typical of numerous small gold and silver mines in Arizona: each flourished for a while, then died. Nothing resembling a Mother Lode or a Comstock Lode was found in Arizona. The mining fortunes that were made, were made in copper.

Despite their lack of spectacular success, the early mining camps in Arizona did much to help settle the state in the last half of the nineteenth century.

It took hard, back-breaking work to dig for gold. These picks at the Gold King Mine (*above*) attest to years of hard usage.
On the side of a hill, a miner's cabin (*opposite*) seems about to give up the ghost. The "ghost" on the porch, incidentally is a whimsical scarecrow.

*This wooden structure (**above**) was called a headframe or gallows frame. Erected over the top of a shaft, it was used to raise and lower ore buckets from the mine. Don Robertson (**below**) explains the workings of an early mine engine. The star performer at the Gold King Mine is this resplendent peacock (**opposite**). He takes pleasure in flashing visitors.*

Tortilla Flat

Along the old Apache Trail, gold was discovered in the late 1800's. The big years at Tortilla Flat were from 1892 to 1897, a dozen mines operating in the area produced $1.5 million in gold. At that time, the trail was lined with saloons, gambling houses, and stores. Since 1950, sporadic mining in the area has produced another $750,000 in gold. But except for the tourists who stop on a drive through the mountains east of Phoenix, things are quiet, and it is doubtful that the present population of 22 is due for a sizable increase.

Tortilla Flat grew up in Indian country. There is no record of a raid, but the danger of one was always there. After the Mexican War, Americans inherited the Spaniards' Indian problem—problems that would persist until the end of the century. The two major tribes that plagued the settlers were the Navahos and the Apaches. There was a vicious circle of raid and retaliation, then another raid in retaliation for the retaliation—a pattern punctuated periodically by uneasy truces.

The Navahos, led by Chiefs Barboncito and Manuelito, surrendered to the Americans in 1866, but it was to be another 20 years before the U.S. Cavalry subdued first Cochise, then Geronimo, of the Apaches. The Apaches were hunters, not farmers like the Hopis. They lived in tepees, not villages like the Pueblos. The Apaches were a proud people who suffered greatly at the hands of the white man. When they went on the warpath, "*Apaches!*" became the most frightening word in the territory. Consider Nana, an old and sickly chief who led 40 Apache braves on a two-month, thousand-mile rampage in 1881. The braves killed 40 whites, wounded another 100, won 8 pitched battles, captured 200 horses, eluded 1,400 troopers and armed civilians, finally escaping to a Mexican hideaway without losing a man.

Until the Indian wars were finally over, the Apaches cast a long shadow across the entire Southwest.

New buildings can be made to look alike, but every old building has its own particular way of falling apart. This one* (opposite) *has received some slapdash repairs, but still seems headed for the terminal stage.
An old beer advertising sign* (above) *at Tortilla Flat slowly is losing its patriotic vivacity.

ASSAY OFFICE
CUSTOM Made LEATHER

Dutchman Gold Mine

spite the sign (**opposite**), *this is the entrance to the Bluebird Mine—not the Lost Dutchman. The Lost Dutchman, people believe, is the Superstition Mountains a few miles away. The old freight depot* (**above**) *and a decaying saddle* (**below**) *attest to the age of rtilla Flat.*

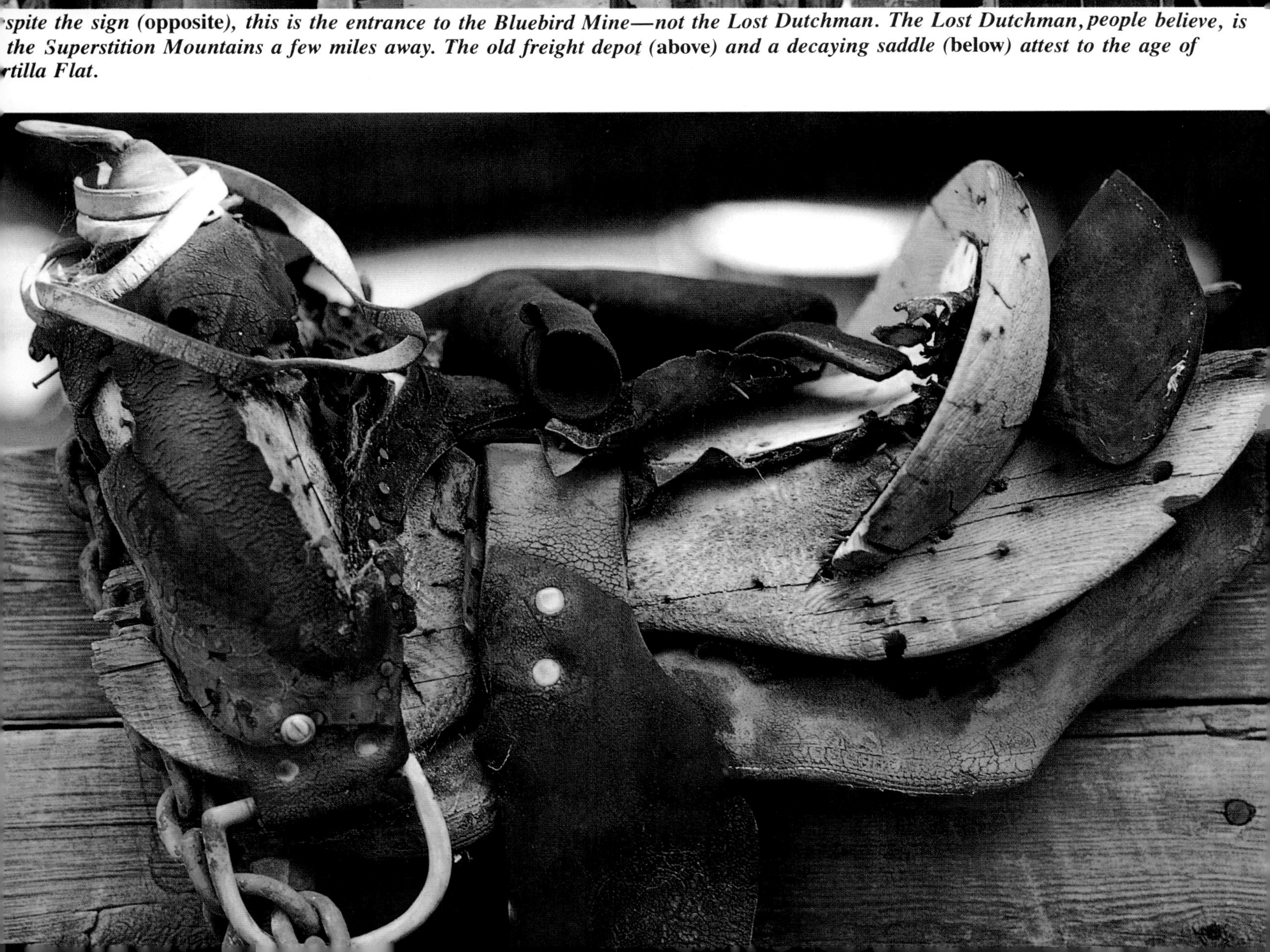

Superstition Mountains

Indians had told Coronado of gold in these rugged mountains, but after several members of his party were killed here under mysterious circumstances he called off the search, naming them the Superstition Mountains. In 1845, Don Miguel Peralta of Senora, Mexico, discovered a rich vein here but he and all his miners were massacred by Apaches. They belived that the miners were defiling the home of their Thunder God.

A Dutch miner later learned the location of the mine from an Apache maiden who was killed by her tribe for her indiscretion. He became a recluse in Phoenix, going into the mountains to bring out ore. Many tried to follow him but he either lost them in the maze of overgrown canyons and gullies or killed them if they got too close. His mine became famous as the Lost Dutchman Mine. Since his death in 1891, many attempts have been made to find the Lost Dutchman but all have failed.

Cactus flowers* (above) *lend a deceptively cheery note to the mountains.
From this angle,* (opposite) *the Superstition Mountains look like a single mountain. Actually, they slope up from the other side in an almost impenetrable maze of gullies and canyons.

Old Tucson

It is ironic that the quintessential Western town, Old Tucson, was created by Hollywood as a set for a movie that almost didn't get made. Columbia Pictures build Old Tucson as the setting for the first big outdoor movie of its time, *Arizona,* starring Jean Arthur and a handsome newcomer, William Holden. Miss Arthur played the role of Phoebe Titus, a brave frontier woman who ran a pie shop, a freight line, and a cattle business while coping with wild Indians, desperadoes, and a land-grabbing, back-shooting villain who had designs on her.

Columbia set designers studied old maps and photographs, and, with the counsel of the Arizona Pioneers Historical Society, they laid out stores, houses, saloons, a mission church, and other buildings to conform exactly with how Tucson looked in the 1860's. Even the streets ran in the same direction. Construction began in July 1939 and was nearly finished when World War II began two months later. The timing practically eliminated the foreign market for the film, and Columbia halted work on the set. The studio changed its mind a few months later, and the set was finished.

When filming was about to begin, 35 professional actors arrived, augmented by 64 Mexicans, 88 Indians, and 18 Anglos for crowd scenes. There also were 43 wranglers, publicity men, first-aid attendants, interpreters (many of the extras couldn't speak English), and a Humane Society official to oversee the treatment of the herds of cattle, horses, and other livestock that completed the setting. The filming of *Arizona* was completed by mid-June 1940. When the movie had its world premiere in Tucson, there were ten thousand invited guests. The public interest was so intense that additional prints of *Arizona* were flown in and shown around the clock in several locations to accommodate the crowds.

For nearly twenty years the set lay abandoned, until promoter Bob Shelton took it over and expanded it as a movie location and developed a family amusement park around it. Since then, more than a hundred

A silhouette of an old-time motion picture camera (**above**) *is an appropriate symbol for the setting of hundreds of movies. The action heats up* (**opposite**) *as two desperados get ready to shoot their way out of a robbery. Old-time gunfights are a popular feature of Old Tucson.*

Old Tucson is authentic down to such small details as this kerosene lamp (above). A little schoolhouse (below) only needs a schoolmarm and some pupils for the cameras to roll. The schoolhouse was featured in an episode of **Little House on the Prairie** ***that was filmed here.***

movies, television movies and programs, and commercials have been filmed on this set. Among the movies that were filmed entirely or in part in Old Tucson: John Wayne's *Rio Lobo, The Alamo, McClintock,* and *El Dorado; Gunfight at the O.K. Corral* with Burt Lancaster and Kirk Douglas; *The Badlanders* with Alan Ladd; Lee Marvin's *Monte Walsh;* Paul Newman's *Hombre;* Robert Taylor's *Return of the Gunfighter; Pray for the Wildcats* with Andy Griffith and William Shatner; and Greer Garson's *Strange Lady in Town*. Episodes of the television programs *Gunsmoke, Bonanza, Little House on the Prairie,* and *Have Gun Will Travel* were made in Old Tucson. Little wonder a visitor has the feeling of *déjà vu*.

There's plenty to do and see here—a tour of the sound stage, gunfights re-enacted in the streets, a mini-tour train, a carousel, a ride through a simulated gold mine, a gun museum, and a wax museum. All this has made Old Tucson second only to the Grand Canyon as a first-rate Arizona attraction.

*If the script calls for a family of substance, they can move right into the handsome house (*above*) across the street from the marshal's office. The staged fights aren't limited to gunplay, (*below*) and can include fisticuffs and tossing the villain over the hero's shoulder.*

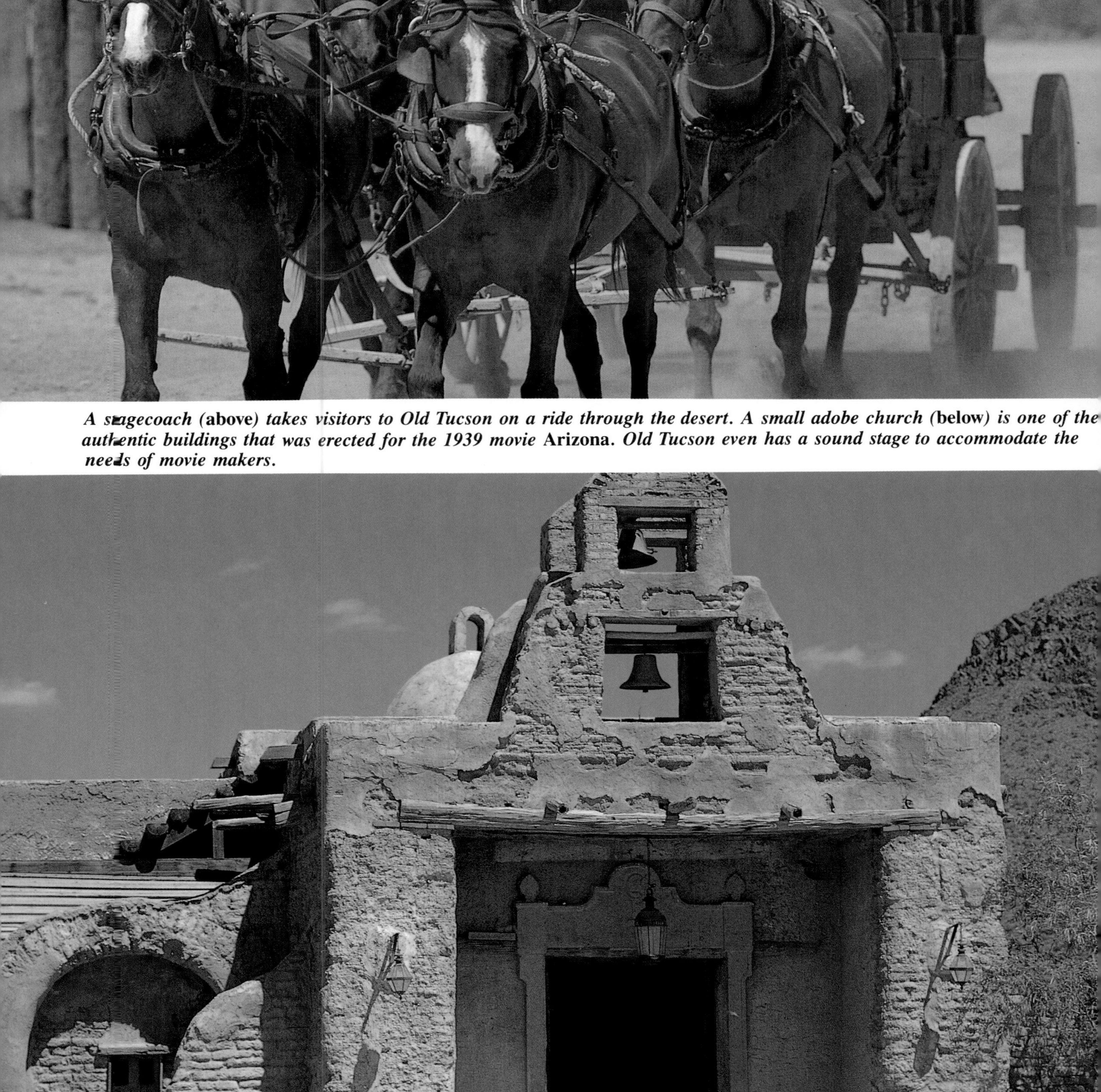

A stagecoach (**above**) *takes visitors to Old Tucson on a ride through the desert. A small adobe church* (**below**) *is one of the authentic buildings that was erected for the 1939 movie* **Arizona**. *Old Tucson even has a sound stage to accommodate the needs of movie makers.*

No Western town would be complete without a mini-mart for the needs of horses and horsemen (**above**). *The main street of this elaborate movie set was designed in its entirety by Hollywood art directors. Every vista* (**below**) *was put together with the camera in mind.*

A tough-looking cowboy strides down the main street of Old Tucson (**above**)*. Actually, he's one of the skilled stuntmen who stage gunfights for visitors. A life-like dummy at the depot* (**below**) *looks as if he just came in from Poisun Well. An old-time locomotive* (**opposite**) *waits at the depot.*

UCSON
11
11
BALDWIN
PHILADELPHIA

Tombstone

He had searched in vain in California and Nevada, and now Ed Schieffelin was prospecting for silver in Apache country in southern Arizona. When soldiers stationed nearby heard what he was doing, they laughed. One told him, "All you're going to find there is your tombstone."

But Schieffelin found not one, but several rich veins, and he took pleasure in naming his first claim "The Tombstone." And unlike many other prospectors, he managed to hold onto his claims, develop them, and grow rich.

Tombstone grew rapidly and so did its reputation as a wide-open town. Many of the men who were attracted to Tombstone had little interest in mining—Wyatt Earp, Doc Holliday, Bat Masterson, and the Clantons and McLowerys.

Much of Tombstone's fame stems from an incident on October 27, 1881. There was bad blood between the Earp brothers and the Clanton and McLowery families. Marshall Earp decided to settle it once and for all. He, his brothers, and Doc Holliday confronted the Clantons and McLowerys at the O.K. Corral, ordering them to throw down their guns. Frank McLowery drew on Earp—who shot him. A barrage of gunfire followed, leaving three of the Clantons and McLowerys dead. Only Doc Holliday was left uninjured.

By 1890, Tombstone had a population of fifteen thousand, but by the turn of the century the mines were playing out and closed for good in 1914.

Tombstone was called, "The Town Too Tough To Die"—and it never really did. It survived, after a fashion, because its reputation was to prove an irresistable attraction to tourists. Those who know its history, will be amused by the marker at Ed Schieffelin's grave. It is inscribed: "This is my Tombstone."

The hangman's noose* (above) *at the Tombstone courthouse saw much use in the days when this was considered the toughest town in the West.
The Tombstone Epitaph (opposite) *was founded in 1880, and still is publishing.*

THE TOMBSTONE EPITAPH
& PROSPECTOR
FOUNDED MAY 1, 1880 BY JOHN P. CLUM
OMBSTONE
PITAPH

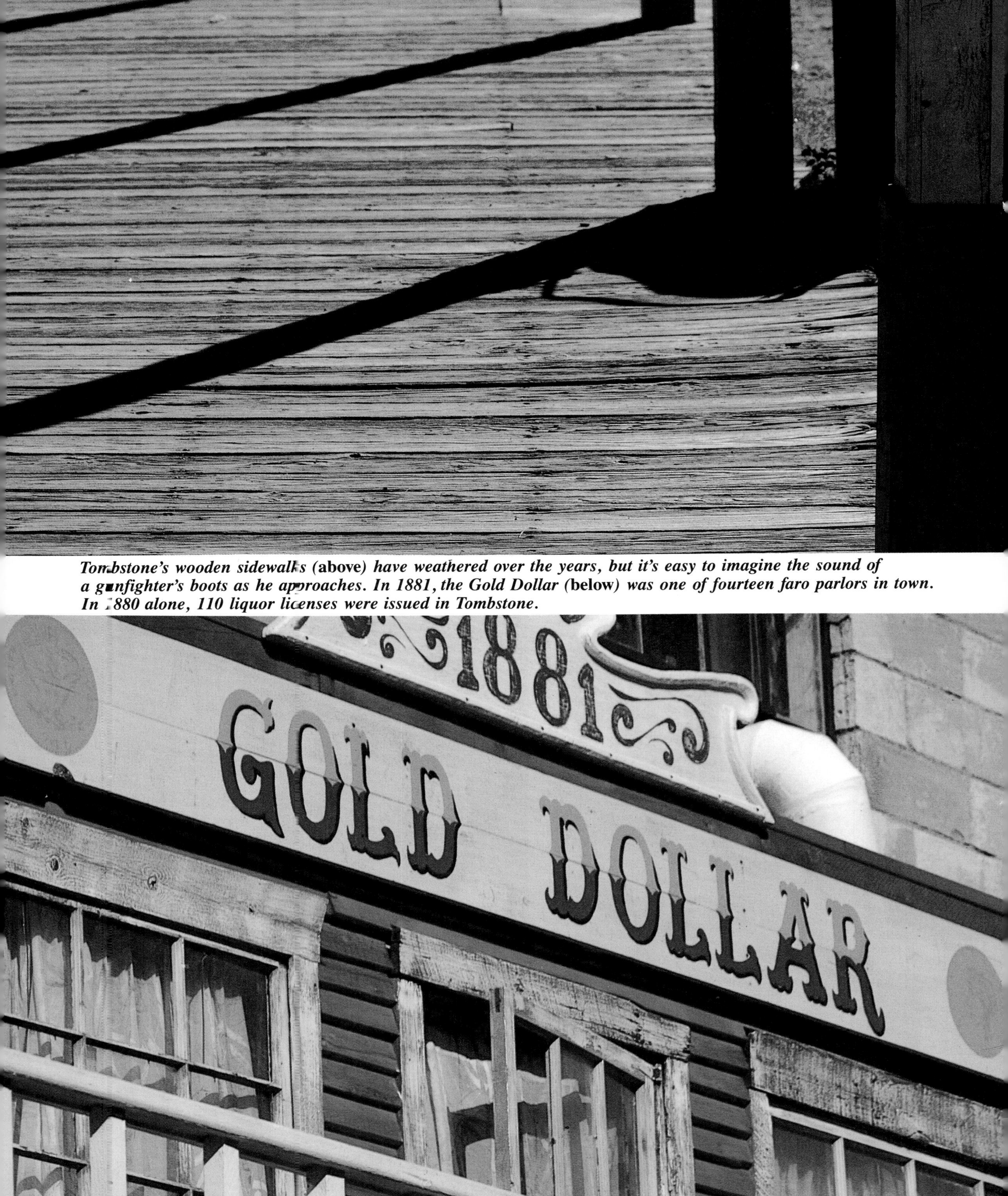

Tombstone's wooden sidewalks (above) have weathered over the years, but it's easy to imagine the sound of a gunfighter's boots as he approaches. In 1881, the Gold Dollar (below) was one of fourteen faro parlors in town. In 1880 alone, 110 liquor licenses were issued in Tombstone.

*Prostitutes were plentiful in the old days, but probably none were as attractive as the lady represented in stained glass (***above***). One of Tombstone's famous madams, Dutch Annie, built her brothel on land leased from Wyatt Earp. A peaceful scene at sunset (***below***).*

The gunfight at the O.K. Corral didn't end the feud, as the sign (**above**) *testifies.*
The best entertainment in town—and the best-looking prostitutes— were to be found at the Bird Cage Theatre (**below**).
In Tombstone, money came and went with great speed.

In the O.K. Corral, life-sized figures (**above**) *show where the participants in the shoot-out stood. It doesn't seem to bother anyone, that the fight took place outside on the street. A vintage crap table* (**below**) *is one of the exhibits at the Bird Cage Theatre.*

HERE
LIES
LESTER MOORE
FOUR SLUGS
FROM A-44
NO LES
NO MORE

Markers in Boot Hill are reproductions. Souvenir hunters got the originals years ago. The stage coach is authentic.

Gleeson

Turquoise was mined in Gleeson for centuries by the Apaches and their ancestors. When the Spaniards came they enslaved the Indians, but never were able to make them tell where the real gem-quality, blue-green stones that the Indians wore could be found. The Spanish mines, worked by Indians, never produced high-quality stones.

By the time Arizona became a territory, the Apaches had learned not to trust the white man. Chief Cochise had promised the Army that the Apaches would be friendly provided they were left alone in their home in the Dragoon Mountains near Gleeson. In 1860, the Army arrested Cochise for a raid on a ranch in this area. He protested his innocence and when he wasn't believed, he escaped. Enraged, he went on the warpath, and for ten years no one in the area was safe from marauding Apaches.

The one white man Cochise trusted was Tom Jeffords, who ran a stage coach station near the Dragoons. After losing twenty-two of his men to Apache raids, Jeffords rode alone to Cochise's camp in the mountains to try to make peace. Cochise was sufficiently impressed with his bravery to make Jeffords a blood brother. Jeffords was able to get Cochise to negotiate with General Howard. A peace treaty was signed and, at the insistence of Cochise, Jeffords was made an Indian agent.

Cochise died shortly after the treaty was signed, and was buried in the Dragoons. Jeffords was the only white man who knew where the burial site was—a secret he took to the grave with him forty years later.

When peace came, turquoise, gold, and silver were mined in the Dragoons, but never in large quantities. Gleeson became the town near the mines. The mines never were more than moderately profitable, and a worsening shortage of water drove the ranchers out of the area. Gleeson slowly withered away.

A sign in the desert* (above) *chronicles the decline and fall of Gleeson. An impressive arch* (opposite) *has outlasted the building it graced. Some years ago Tiffany & Co., the New York jeweler, announced plans to finance large-scale mining of turquoise near Gleeson, but some preliminary mining failed to find a sufficient yield of gem-quality stones, and the plans were abandoned.

A prairie dog (**above**) *surveys the situation near Gleeson, probably wondering where all the people went. A building in town* (**below**) *slowly is giving way to the elements. Gleeson was named for one of the early miners in the area.*

A desolate scene (**above**) *across the prairie, where Apaches once terrorized isolated ranchers. Live oaks shade a store in Gleeson* (**below**)*. The Apaches gathered* **beyotas**, *the edible acorns of the oak. The road to Gleeson now is in disrepair.*

Bisbee

The mine is on one side of Tombstone Canyon, the town on the other, clinging to the steep slope in a haphazard manner. The public buildings line the main street at the bottom of the slope.

Copper was discovered here in 1877 by an Indian scout named Jack Dunn, who with his partner, George Warren, founded the Copper Queen Mine. Phelps Dodge purchased land nearby, and to avoid legal problems over mining

A larger-than-life statue of a copper miner (**above**) *overlooks the main street of Bisbee.*

The sides of the canyon rise steeply, and winding roads head off in every direction from downtown* (opposite)*. A museum in the old mine offices demonstrates the intricate process of mining copper.

claims, the two companies merged to form the Copper Queen Consolidated Mining Company. They named the town Bisbee after an Eastern stockholder, who, incidentally, never visited his namesake.

The mine was a big producer by 1885, and continued large-scale operations until 1975—a record of longevity few mines in the country can equal. The depressed price of copper closed the mine; but an upward swing in the price may see a reopening of the Copper Queen.

In the meantime, Bisbee waits. It is a semi-ghost town, but it has attracted a number of young people who are building a life of their own in the old buildings.

A relic of the past is the historic Copper Queen Hotel, still welcoming guests. It is a short walk from the hotel to most of the important buildings and sites in town.

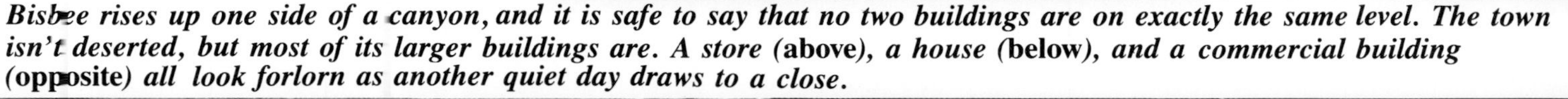

Bisbee rises up one side of a canyon, and it is safe to say that no two buildings are on exactly the same level. The town isn't deserted, but most of its larger buildings are. A store (**above**)*, a house* (**below**)*, and a commercial building* (**opposite**) *all look forlorn as another quiet day draws to a close.*

NEW MEXICO

The Indians were hostile and so was the environment. Silver had been found by the Spanish south of Santa Fe. There was gold, too, but never enough to sustain a boom. That would come with the discovery of uranium.

Madrid

Not silver, not gold, but coal made Madrid a boom town. The town was particularly fortunate. This is one of the few places in the world where hard (anthracite) and soft (bituminous) coal have been found together; and one of three places in the country where hard coal has been found.

As early as 1835, Madrid was supplying coal to a gold mine at Dolores, three miles away. In the Mexican War, General Stephen Watts Kearny, the conqueror of New Mexico, used Madrid coal for his army. Ox teams once hauled coal from Madrid into St. Louis.

Miners worked small mines in Madrid until the Atchison, Topeka & Santa Fe Railroad came. In 1889, the railroad built a spur line to the mines. By the end of the century, three thousand Madrid miners were producing coal for the Santa Fe Railroad and to heat homes throughout the Southwest, and the mines had been consolidated into a single company.

A typical company town grew up at Madrid. Four long rows of identical houses faced the company store, mine offices, and other commercial buildings. The miners were expected to spend their wages at the company store, which had a limited array of goods. The women would get more interesting items from mail-order houses, sneaking the packages home so company officials wouldn't see them. One doctor looked after the miners and their families. The miners were charged a dollar a month for medical expenses, although that didn't include the expense of delivering babies.

Oscar Huber came to Madrid in 1910 and rose steadily in the company, getting control of the mines in 1938. He made a profound change in the town, providing an ample water supply, building a hospital and good schools, paving the roads, and sponsoring a baseball team with its own ball park.

An entrance to the coal mine (**above**) *has crumbled over the years. Company houses* (**opposite**) *stand empty, facing the deserted company story. For years, these houses had neither electricity or sufficient water.*

Coal was brought from the mines on wooden cars (**above**)*. When the Santa Fe tore up the tracks on its spur line to Madrid, it had forgotten that there was an engine at the mine* (**below**) *where it still sits today. The old mines and equipment now are a museum and attract many visitors.*

This truck (above) *has made its last run, and sits patiently by the mine. It's hard to believe that Madrid once had a wide reputation for its gala Christmas displays. Every miner's house* (below) *was draped with colored lights. At the annual lighting ceremony, the people sang* **Let There Be Light**.

A coal miner's house in Madrid (**above**) *and a house of one of the foremen* (**below**). *Neither suggests that a miner's life above ground was too much more pleasant than his life below ground. It was a big event when the houses were electrified.*

*What once was the company store (*above*) now caters to visitors to the old mine. Most all the buildings in town are now showing the effect of years of neglect (*below*). The company was very paternalistic; for years the mine fielded a baseball team.*

A forlorn row of company houses faces the old coal mine at Madrid.

Dos Cabezas

Spanish conquistadors named the twin granite mountains Dos Cabezas (two heads), when they came by in the 1550's in search of the fabled seven cities of gold. After the Mexican War, a spring was found here and Dos Cabezas became a stage coach line station. This was Apache country, and in the first eighteen months of operation sixteen stages were ambushed, their drivers and passengers slain. The line was shut down and was reopened a few years later by John Butterfield, the most successful stage coach operator in the Southwest.

Prospectors stopping at Dos Cabezas found ore deposits nearby, and a town grew up. About 1906, a rich vein of copper was found by a prospector known as "Old Man" Mitchell. He sold his claim to T.N. McCauley, who organized backing and formed the Mascot Copper Company, Ltd. The company installed modern equipment, recruited miners, built a smelter and a railhead to Dos Cabezas.

The town prospered for twenty years. There was brisk trading in Little Mascot stock. The company continued to expand. But just as a new generating plant was completed, the Little Mascot played out. Surveys were made, new mines dug, hundreds of samples were assayed, but the mining days at Dos Cabezas were over. More than three hundred employees were laid off and told to leave town if they could. Most of the major buildings were torn down.

A few families stayed on, but their number dwindled as the years passed. Dos Cabezas is a true ghost town today, its adobe buildings slowly crumbling in the desert.

An old wagon* (above) *is a reminder of the time when mining turned a stage coach stop into a thriving town.

This adobe ruin* (opposite) *was the general store in Dos Cabezas. When the Little Mascot mine was in operation, the town had a grade school, dancehall, churches, a dairy—even a movie theater.

White Oaks

California hadn't been lucky for John Baxter, but he didn't stop looking for gold. He learned from a bartender that some gold had been found near the springs here, and he and two others went in search of it. They found a little. Baxter and his remaining partner later sold their Homestake claim for $300,000—a mine that was to yield more than three million.

By 1887, White Oaks had grown to four thousand people. The only thing their town lacked, the citizens felt, was a railroad

White Oaks assumed that a railroad would have to come through town. Why, the town even had a coal mine. And when the Kansas City, El Paso, and Mexican Railway showed interest, White Oaks assumed they would pay top dollar for the privilege and the town set its right-of-way prices accordingly. The railroad protested the prices, White Oaks refused to compromise, and the railroad went to Carrizozo instead.

The mines began to falter in the 1890's, and when the mines went—White Oaks died.

***A decorated skull of a steer* (above) *hangs over the door of one of the few remaining buildings in White Oaks. This is what is left of the Exchange Bank of White Oaks* (opposite).**

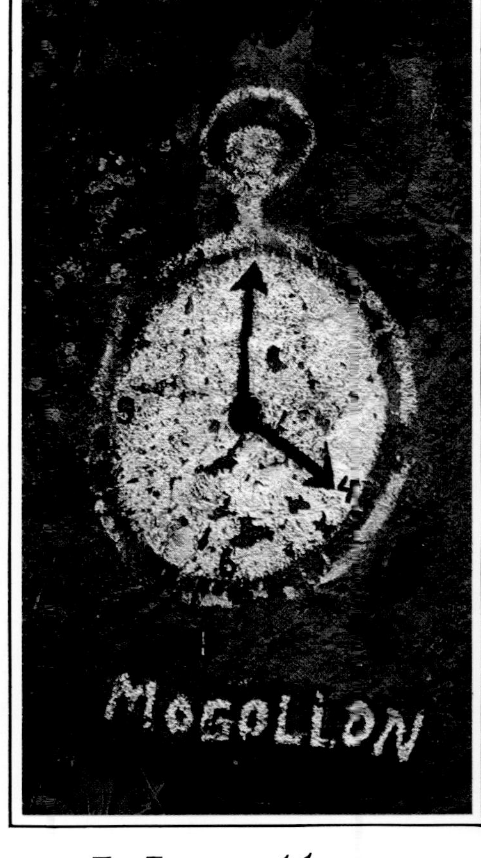

Mogollon

In the late 1860's, U.S. Cavalry Sergeant James Cooney was on a scouting expedition when he discovered rock ledges rich in gold ore in a canyon near Mogollon. He told no one, and when he was discharged in 1876 he gathered some friends to begin mining. The Apaches drove off the party, but they came back two years later and restaked their claims. Trouble with the Apaches persisted, however, particularly after the miners killed the son-in-law of the great Chief Victorio. The Indians besieged the miners, but were driven off. Cooney and a friend then set off to warn other settlers, only to be ambushed and killed.

Cooney's brother Michael came to take over the claims and was a force in developing the district, including mines at Silver Creek—

The significance of the watch* (above) *painted on a wall has been lost over the years. The general store* (opposite) *also was the blacksmith shop, and the center of social life in Mogollon.

BLACKSMITH
STORE

There's a little life in the old town yet. In the summer the theater (above) *shows old movies. This house* (below) *has slipped beyond repair. An unconfirmed story has it that Butch Cassidy, the Sundance Kid, and their gang once spent a winter in this remote mining town in the mountains.*

One of the old mine buildings (**above**) *apparently was later used by a tobacconist. The canyon wall rises sharply behind this miner's shack* (**below**). *Many of the miners here were Mexicans, and the 5th of May, Mexico's Independence Day, was celebrated with a parade down the town's one street.*

where the town of Mogollon (pronounced locally as *muggy-own*) was founded. A big strike here came in 1889, and Mogollon became the most important settlement in the mountains. The mine was the Little Fanny, and it helped the area produce eighteen million ounces of silver over the years—a quarter of the state's total production. A later strike was brought in by Ernest Craig, an English mining engineer. He returned to England a wealthy man, and later was elected to the House of Commons.

Mogollon was an important silver-producing town until the 1930's. Mining continued until the end of World War II, then stopped. In recent years, a few artists have moved here, but the aura of a ghost town still clings to Mogollon.

Pinos Altos

Some believe that the Spaniards panned gold here as early as 1800, but were massacred by Apaches, and some old adobe ruins tend to bear that story out. But the real history of Pinos Altos starts in 1860, when a man known as Three-Fingered Birch and two companions found gold in Bear Creek. In a few months, some seven hundred men were panning gold in the stream.

In December 1860, the first gold vein was struck, which was to become known as the Pacific Vein. The only problem at Pinos Altos was that the Apaches were still killing miners in ambushes. The mining camp was smack in the middle of Apache hunting grounds, and the Apaches had no intention of letting it stay there.

The Apache chief Red Sleeves rode up to the camp one day and said if the miners would leave, he would lead them to a great gold deposit to the south. The miners seized Red Sleeves, gave him a horsewhipping, and threw him out of their camp. Red Sleeves took his grievances to Cochise, and they agreed to jointly attack the mining camp. At dawn, September 28, 1861, four hundred

The blossoms of a cactus at Pinos Altos* (above) *are as red as the blood shed in the skirmishes with the Apaches.
The opera house* (opposite) *suggests that life in the mining camp had its moments of relaxation.

Apaches attacked. But, the miners were ready for them and drove them off after a pitched battle. Fifteen Apaches and three miners were killed, seven miners were wounded.

Other raids followed, and it wasn't until 1874 that peace came. The miners and the Apaches agreed that a large wooden cross would be erected on a hilltop overlooking the town, and that as long as the cross stood, there would be no more trouble.

By the 1890's, Pinos Altos had grown into a sizeable town, boasting two hotels, a drugstore, and even a Turkish bath. In 1906, a narrow-gauge railroad reached town to transport ore to the Silver City smelters. The mines were wearing out, however, and Pinos Altos slowly wound down to almost a ghost town.

The Buckhorn (**above**) *was the scene of many a drunken brawl. The general store* (**below**) *is open again, although its offerings are sharply limited. A cat* (**opposite**) *keeps an eye on what's left of an old home in Pinos Altos. George Hearst owned mines here and when he sold out in 1906, others followed suit.*

Shakespeare

During its lifetime, this town south of Lordsburg had more ups and downs than a jack-in-the-box. At first it was called Mexican Springs, for the fresh water that made it a stop for covered wagons heading for California. When John Butterworth started his Overland Mail in 1858, linking St. Louis and San Francisco, Mexican Springs became a mail stop and people started to settle here.

A prospector named W.D. Brown stopped and found some promising ore in the nearby Pyramid Mountains. He took his samples to San Francisco and was able to get in and show them to William C. Ralston, the organizer of the Bank of California. An assay report showed a whopping twelve thousand ounces of silver to the ton. Ralston set out for Grant to see for himself. He laid out the Virginia Mining District covering 120 square miles, and planned a town which he modestly named Ralston City.

But there was trouble afoot. Prospectors found that Ralston's men had staked out all the choice claims. Some sued, many left. The scheme fell apart, and the town was as small as it ever was.

A few years later an improbable pair, Philip Arnold and John Slack, showed up at Ralston's bank with diamonds they said they found in the Ralston City area. Tiffany's pronounced the stones genuine, and Ralston sent a mining expert to investigate. He found diamonds vouched for the claim. Ralston bought Arnold and Slack out for $600,000, and started to promote stock in the project. Prospectors flocked to the site. The scheme came tumbling down when a cut stone was found. The area had been salted by Arnold and Slack, who were nowhere to be found.

Since 1933, what's left of Shakespeare has been owned by the Hill family. Several times they have tried to make it a commercial attraction, but they haven't been successful. The Hills' daughter and her husband ranch the area, and give tours of Shakespeare on Sundays.

*A ranch horse (***above***) is one of the few current residents of this ghost town. A view down the main street (***opposite***). Once such outlaws as Jim Ringo and Curly Bill Brocius walked here.*

During Shakespeare's short boom, solid adobe buildings (above) *were built along its one street. From the hill behind the town, a horse is the only sign of life* (below). *The Hill family, the owners of Shakespeare, give Sunday tours and use the admission fees to pay for maintenance.*

The relics of the past crowd the porch of what was once the town's general store (above). *The hills near Shakespeare* (below) *were once salted with diamonds, a ruse that might have worked if the con men hadn't used a few cut stones. Several such scams gave the town a bad reputation.*

Lincoln

This sleepy New Mexico town is haunted by the ghost of its most notorious citizen. His real name was Henry McCarty. He was born in New York City. When his father died, the family settled in Silver City, New Mexico. He killed a man when he was 15 and fled to Lincoln, using the name of his stepfather, William Bonney. A rancher befriended him and gave him a job. When the rancher was slain in the Lincoln County cattle war, Bonney, now known as Billy the Kid, went on a rampage. His career of rustling and killing had begun.

Billy the Kid was arrested in Lincoln and charged with three murders. He escaped, killing a deputy. He was recaptured, tried and convicted but escaped again, this time killing two deputies. At that time, Billy boasted that he had twenty-one notches on his gun handle, one killing for each year he had lived.

Pat Garrett became sheriff of Lincoln County in 1880, and later that year found Billy the Kid at a ranch near Fort Sumner, surprised him in his bedroom, and killed him in the ensuing gun fight.

A carved likeness of Billy the Kid is memorabilia of this infamous man. A church near Lincoln* (opposite) *is a reminder of the area's Spanish heritage.

LA IGLESIA
DE
SAN JUAN BAUTISTA

Making his escape, Billy the Kid shot a deputy sheriff to death from the second-story window of the courthouse (above). The post office at Lincoln (below). At the time of the cattle war, Lincoln County was approximately the same size as the state of Connecticut.

The head stone of Billy the Kid and his "pals" in the Lincoln cemetery (**above**). *The stone once was stolen, but later recovered. Souvenir hunters have chipped off part of the right side. It now is protected by a fence. The legend of the Kid grew in places like the saloon* (**below**).

Fort Union

Fort Union sprang into being in 1851 to protect travelers on the Santa Fe Trail, and was left to crumble in the desert sun in 1890—after the last of the Indian Wars was over. Today it is both a national monument, and an intriguing ghost town. For Fort Union was a town, albeit not an orthodox one. Officer's wives lived here, children were born in the fort's hospital, attended the small school, grew up, and got married at the church. There was a trading post, and a jail. True, there was no mine, but there were plenty of horses and guns, and a rigid, sometimes harsh, discipline that no mining camp ever would have tolerated.

For the horse soldier, life on the frontier was a ceaseless round of drills, hard work, bad food, tedium, and boredom—punctuated with forrays and skirmishes that never seemed to settle anything. The bugle blew at five o'clock a.m. and called the soldier practically every hour after that to new duties and chores—target practice, cavalry drills, stable police, and often such non-military jobs as grading roads and stringing telegraph labor. For this, and for fighting Indians, a private was paid $13 a month. He also had to endure the extremes of heat and cold in a land where, one soldier wrote, "everything that grows pricks and everything that breathes bites."

For many soldiers, it was almost a relief to go into action. When the regiment went on a campaign, an army wife recalled, the band would escort the cavalry out of the fort to the strains of *The Girl I Left Behind Me*, while the womanfolk tried to hold back their tears. The band greeted the returning soldiers with *Out of the Wilderness*.

The soldiers from Fort Union fought in the final major Indian uprising in the West, when in 1884 Geronimo led the Apaches out of their New Mexico reservation and terrified the Territory. Two years later, Geronimo surrended. An era was over, and Fort Union was soon to become only a memory.

The battle flag of the Eighth Cavalry **(above)** *is proudly displayed in the fort's small museum.*
Through this gate, **(opposite)** *the regiment would ride out on a campaign as the band played.*

Little is left of the officer's quarters at Fort Union, (above) *but a few chimneys and bits of adobe walls. Two decrepit wagons* (below) *await horses that died a century ago. A smooth-bore cannon* (opposite) *was of litte use in fighting Indians. In the last years at Fort Union, Gatling and Hotchkiss guns provided superior firepower.*

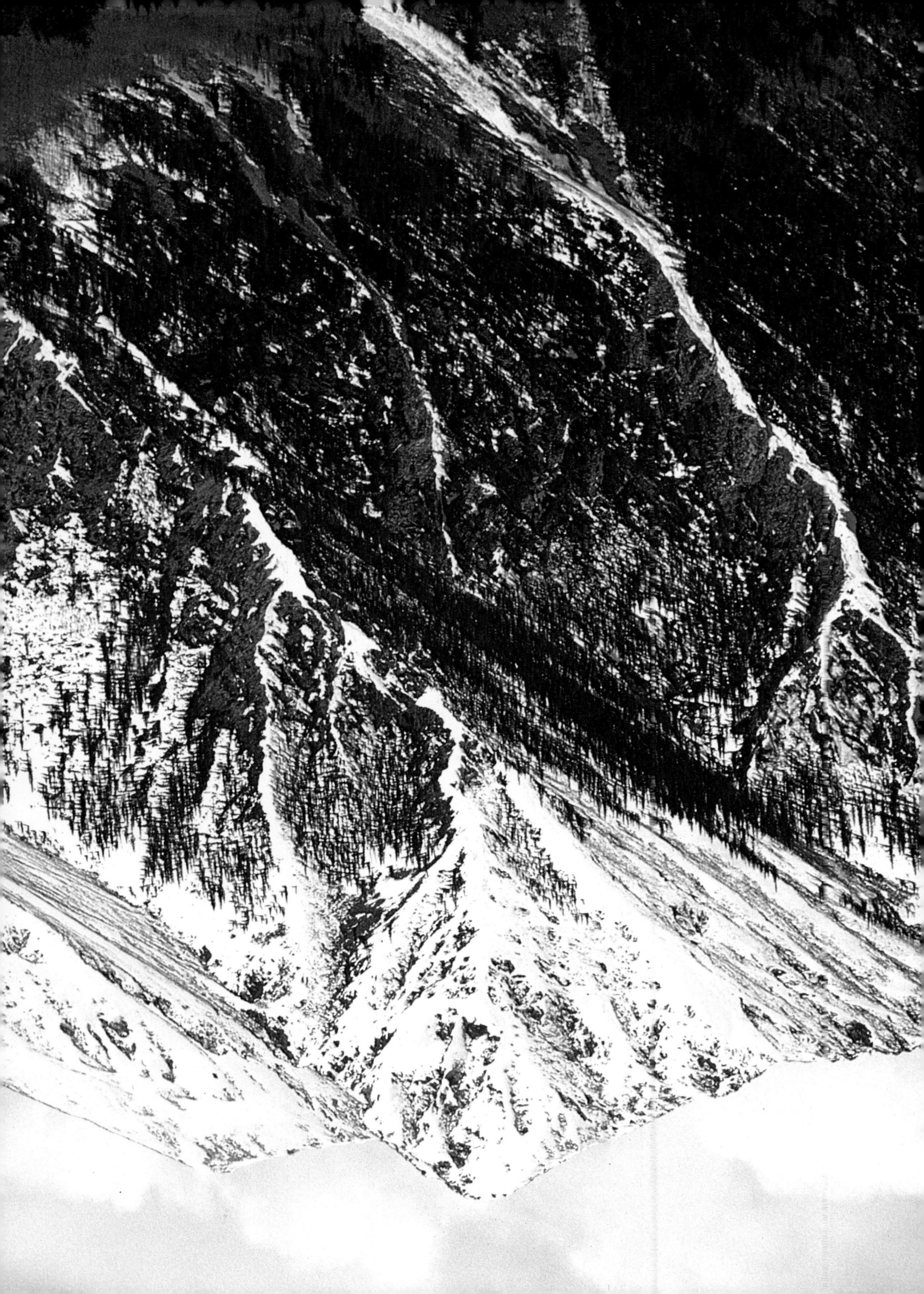

At first, the Rockies were merely obstacles to be crossed on the way to the gold fields. Later, miners were to discover that these mountains held riches beyond compare.

The
OLD HOMESTEAD
..... LAST OF
CRIPPLE CREEK'S NOTORIOUS
PARLOUR HOUSES
NOW ON DISPLAY
GUIDED TOURS OF 10 ROOMS

Cripple Creek

Should this famous mining town south of Pike's Peak need a motto, none would be more appropriate than *In Vino Veritas;* for it was the vision of a young man with a severe drinking problem that led to the gold strike here—one of the richest the world has ever known.

Bob Womack was brought to Colorado by his father in 1861 to avoid conscription in the Civil War, and to hunt for gold. They had a small silver mine near Georgetown for awhile, but the father felt his health was being impaired by mining, sold the mine and bought a cattle ranch nearby. Bob Womack hated ranching and spent most of his time drinking. He would tell anyone who would listen, that he believed there were rich lodes of gold in Cripple Creek.

One day the young man found some rocks that assayed at $200 a ton. People discounted his find; Womack wasn't reliable and a gold hoax here a few years before still haunted them. A dentist loaned him $600 and he found a still lode, but he still wasn't taken seriously. A German count living in Colorado Springs, James Pourtales, decided to try his hand at mining and struck gold not far from the Womack mine. This was the seal of approval everyone was waiting for. Cripple Creek became a boom town practically overnight.

By 1889, Cripple Creek mines had produced $21 million in gold. A devastating fire practically leveled Cripple Creek in 1896, but it was quickly rebuilt—this time of brick. The mines produced $23 million in 1900 alone. By then Cripple Creek was a city, served by seven railroads and an electric trolly system.

Cripple Creek made some thirty millionaires before the boom was over. Bob Womack was not one of them. He died in Colorado Springs in 1909, sixty-six years old and penniless. His unshakable belief in gold at Cripple Creek, though, had led to a $400 million bonanza.

A figure sitting on a scale in a Cripple Creek store window,* (above) *seems to suggest that in the rip-roaring days here, a girl could be worth her weight in gold. If not literally true, certainly the girls at such parlour houses as the Old Homestead* (opposite) *benefited mightily from the bonanza.

Gold is still mined at Cripple Creek as this sign proclaims, (**above**) *but the last major mine here shut down nearly 25 years ago. A battered survivor of the early days,* (**below**) *when miners' shacks covered the nearby hills. Most of the original wooden buildings burned in the fire of 1896.*

Solid brick Victorian buildings (**above**) *line the two major streets in Cripple Creek, which proclaims itself the "world's greatest gold camp"* (**below**). *At one point, the clash between mill owners and miners became so violent that soldiers were called in, and 112 agitators and miners were deported.*

Leadville

Leadville had it all. It was a booming gold camp in 1860. Silver was discovered in 1878, a bonanza that in ten years had produced some $136 million. When the price of silver collapsed in 1893, Leadville returned successfully to gold mining. In this century, lead, zinc, manganese, and molybdenum have been mined in the area. The glory years, though, were the 1880's when Leadville was the silver capital of Colorado. One of the stories from that era bears retelling.

Horace A.W. Tabor was a 47-year-old failed prospector-turned-grocer, when he bought the Matchless Mine in 1878 and struck it rich. It was to net him

The House With the Eye* (above) *is a Leadville landmark. The eye symbolized the all-seeing eye of God. The main street* (opposite) *has changed little over the past century. At 10,500 feet above sea level, Leadville is the highest incorporated city in the United States. Snow usually comes in October, and lingers well into May. Near the Matchless, where Baby Doe Tabor spent the last 35 years of her life as a recluse, the remnants of old mines look dreary in a late spring snow. The Tabors were not the only famous people to come out of Leadville. An Irish lass married a miner here and became the Unsinkable Molly Brown. Leadville also was the birthplace and childhood home of Lowell Thomas.

THE DEE HIVE
GIFT SHOP
VAN TOURS
SOUVENIRS
T-SHIRTS
Happy Trails
BABY DOE
FASHIONS

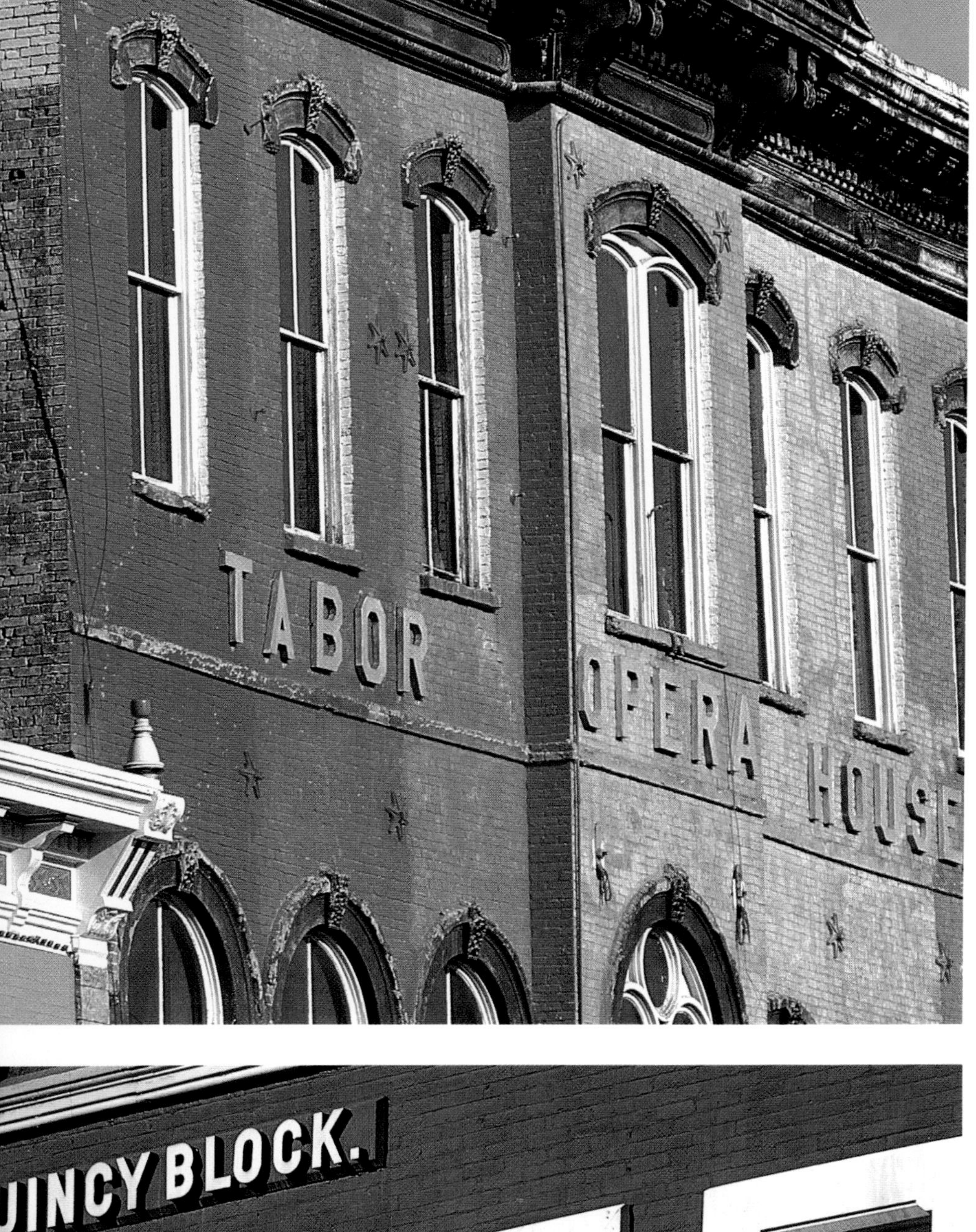

$10 million. Tabor wanted to have a good time, live in the grand manner, and run for political office. His austere wife disapproved. Soon his eye fell on the beautiful Baby Doe McCourt, who recently had separated from her husband. Soon Horace had installed Baby Doe in Denver's finest hotel, as his mistress.

The liaison scandalized Leadville and Denver society, but the couple wasn't bothered. Tabor was busy building an opera house for Denver—the Tabor Grand Theatre—and serving as the state's lieutenant governor. He was elected U.S. Senator in 1883 and, his divorce final, took Baby Doe to Washington with him. They were married in the Willard Hotel and she wore a $7,000 dress. President Chester A. Arthur, many senators, and congressmen were among the guests, but their wives were not. The Tabors were ostracized from Washington society.

A decade of high living and profligate spending followed. Then, President Grover Cleveland demonetized silver and Tabor's empire fell apart. The Matchless was practically worthless, and his other properties were highly mortgaged. At 65, Tabor was back in Leadville working as a laborer for three dollars a day. He died in 1899 and his last words to Baby Doe were, "Hang on to the Matchless. It will make millions again."

And hang on she did, finally moving into a tool shed at the mine. She lived there in poverty until February 1935, when friends found her frozen body on the floor.

Horace Tabor built an opera house (*above*) in Leadville, then a more grandiose one in Denver. Stately rows of Victorian windows (*below*) keep a watch on the doings of Leadville. In the mountains (*left*), Leadville is twice as high as Denver, and has the nickname of Cloud City.

8

Fairplay

A small mining camp named Tarryall sprang up on a stream near the South Platte River in the Rockies. When news of the strike spread, newcomers arrived, but were treated badly by the miners. One bitter group moved on to South Platte itself, where they found gold flakes. They started a camp of their own and named it Fairplay.

When the placer gold was exhausted, the miners were able to raise the money to begin hard-rock diggings. But when the price of gold remained fixed, and the cost of hard-rock mining continued to increase, Fairplay slowly began to fade.

Today Fairplay is a collection of original buildings, buildings moved from other ghost towns in

A little red schoolhouse (**above**) *is a popular attraction in Fairplay. So many early wooden buildings in America were painted red, not for aesthetic reasons, but because red paint was easy to make and was inexpensive. Storefronts* (**opposite**) *recall the days when Fairplay was a thriving community. There were more than thirty saloons and dancehalls, not to mention a dozen brothels.*

STORE

*A b'acksmith (**above**) was vital to an early mining camp in the days when horsepower was generated by Forses, not engines. The streets of Fairplay (**below**) were unpaved and were ankle deep in mud during the spring thaws. Mining camps in the Colorado Rockies suffered hard winters.*

the area, and a few reconstructions. One of the area's ghost towns worth visiting is Buckskin Joe, named after "Buckskin Joe" Higganbottom who led the group of miners who discovered gold there in 1859.

A smallpox epidemic struck Buckskin Joe in the 1860's, and a beautiful dancehall girl named Silverheels nursed the miners, after the other women had fled. The grateful miners wanted to reward her, but she could not be found. She had also contracted smallpox and, her beauty gone, had quietly left town. Mount Silverheels was named in her memory.

*The initials on the train (***above***) mean that it belonged to the Denver, South Park, and Hilltop narrow-gauge line which serviced a number of mining towns. The roofs of these buildings (***below***) are beginning to sag with age, but there still are lace curtains in the windows.*

Silver Plume

The ghost of a young Englishman named Griffin haunts this once bustling mining camp. One of the first to arrive, Griffin discovered the Seven-Thirty mine, rich in both silver and gold. Despite his good fortune, he made no friends, and didn't frequent the saloons or brothels.

A visitor to Silver Plume brought the rumor that the night before Griffin was to have been married in England, his fiancée was found dead in his room. Griffin neither confirmed, nor denied the story.

Shortly after the story was circulated, people noticed that every evening after returning from his mine, Griffin would dig in front of his cabin on the mountain overlooking Silver Plume. Then he would get his violin and play. The music drifted down to the town.

One evening, the music ended and a shot rang out. Some townspeople went to Griffin's cabin to investigate. They found him lying face down, in a self-dug grave. He had killed himself with a bullet in his heart.

Stores from mining camp days* (above) *still cling to the sides of the canyon at Silver Plume.

These once proud facades* (opposite) *are reminders of the days when Silver Plume was booming. Colorado still was a territory. Movements for statehood had failed in 1864, 1865, and 1867. Colorado finally was admitted as the 38th state in 1876. Both Indian wars and the Civil War delayed progress in the territory.

Three major Indian battles were fought in Colorado. Hundreds of Cheyenne and Arapaho were killed by American troops in the 1864 Sand Creek Massacre. Four years later, some one thousand Cheyenne and Sioux besieged federal troops for nine days, in the Battle of Breecher Island. In the Thornburgh Massacre of 1878, Utes ambushed American troops, because they didn't want to be sent to reservations.

OPEN
429

NO
PARKING
THIS
SIDE
NO
PARKING
THIS
SIDE
STOP
Toad's
Tool
Clothing
for

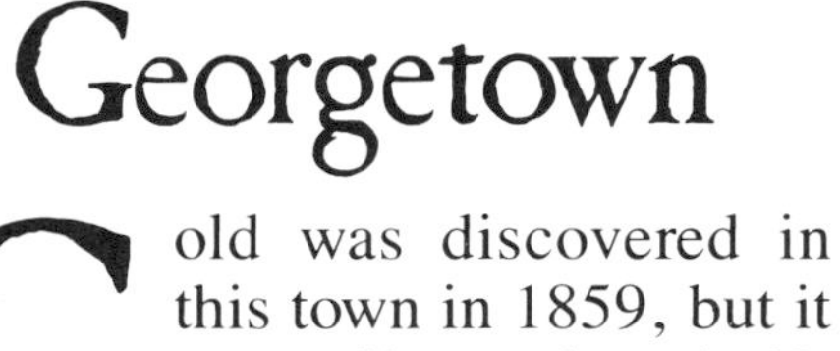

Georgetown

Gold was discovered in this town in 1859, but it was silver that built Georgetown. Until the strike at Leadville in 1878, it was the most important silver camp in the state.

Georgetown was famous through the years for a notable hotel, the Hotel de Paris—the creation of *Louis Dupuy*, a Frenchman who squandered his inheritance before coming to America. He joined the U.S. Army, served in Wyoming, deserted, and took a job with a Denver newspaper as a mine reporter. He quit and became a miner, but was injured in an explosion. He became a cook in Georgetown, eventually bought the bakery in which he worked, and in 1875 opened the doors of his hotel.

The Hotel de Paris was famous throughout the West for its cuisine, its elegant furnishings, and its unusual owner. Only guests who met with Mr. Dupuy's personal approval were allowed to stay in the hotel.

A statue of Justice **(above)** ***adorns the roof of the Hotel de Paris. The main street of Georgetown*** **(opposite)** ***is a model of Victorian charm.***

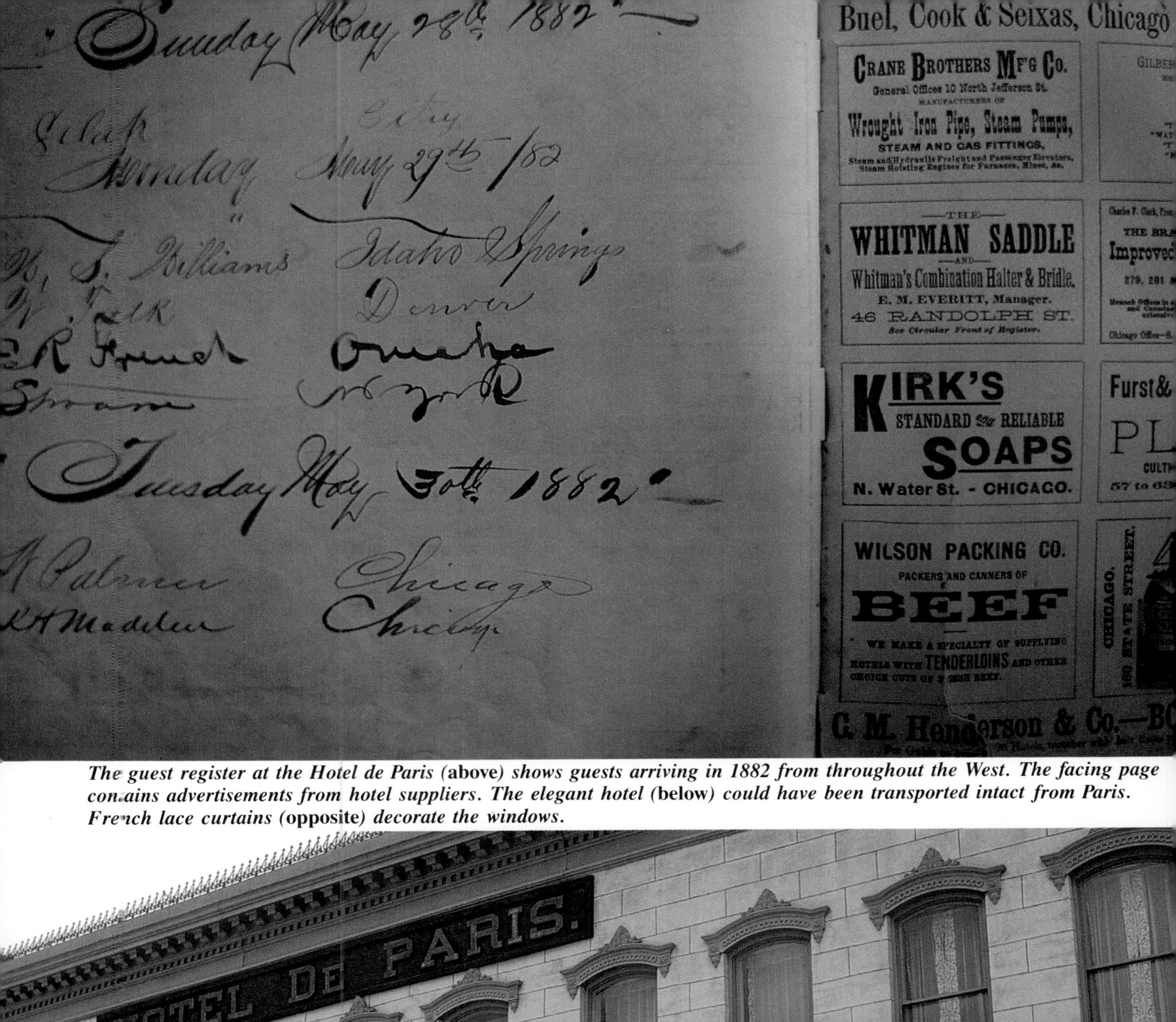

The guest register at the Hotel de Paris (above) shows guests arriving in 1882 from throughout the West. The facing page contains advertisements from hotel suppliers. The elegant hotel (below) could have been transported intact from Paris. French lace curtains (opposite) decorate the windows.

St. Elmo

Three of the highest peaks in central Colorado are Mts. Harvard, Yale, and Princeton. South of Mt. Princeton and just west of the famous Chalk Cliffs are the remains of St. Elmo, a town that sprang up in the early 1880s because of the Mary Murphy mine, and other smaller mines nearby. St. Elmo also was the supply depot when the Denver, South Park and Pacific Railroad dug the Alpine Tunnel to Gunnison.

St. Elmo was the hub of this mining area. Toll roads from here led to Tin Cup, Aspen, and Maysville. In the good old days, the town had a population of more than three hundred. There was a hotel, several saloons, and it was a popular stopover for travelers. There was a five thousand foot tramway from the tunnel outlet to the Mary Murphy mine, which also accommodated passengers.

In 1910, rail traffic through the tunnel was discontinued, and trains in Chalk stopped in 1926. The Mary Murphy stopped operations about this time, after producing some $14 million in gold. St. Elmo was doomed.

All that is left now are a handful of weathering buildings along a narrow, unpaved street. But St. Elmo is a classic ghost town and its mountain setting makes it one of the most attractive in the state.

Spring wildflowers* (above) *bring a spot of bright color to the Rocky Mountain setting of St. Elmo. The main street* (opposite) *of town once was crowded with travelers.* (Overleaf)*, The passage of time is recoloring the buildings of St. Elmo.

Telluride

This old mining town in the mountains of southern Colorado took its name, as any geologist would know, from the ore that abounded in the mountains, a compound containing the non-metallic element tellurium. But the name of the game here in the 1870's was not telluride, but silver.

Despite the beauty of the mountains, life was hard in Telluride. The winters were severe, and the steep mountain sides were not suitable for farming or grazing. Most meat and other foodstuff had to be brought in. Worse, there was a severe and continuing shortage of women. Men outnumbered women about 50-to-1, and while there was an ample supply of houses of prostitution, many men wanted something more permanent. For years, there was a brisk business here in mail order brides.

Telluride was the town chosen for the first unauthorized bank withdrawal made by Butch Cassidy and his gang. As distinctive an honor as that is, another story involving a local bank is much more revealing of the character of Telluride and other mining towns.

In the early 1930s, when the Depression was causing bank failures around the country, the head of a Telluride bank went to New York with papers that he had carefully doctored, and borrowed enough money to pay in full all his bank's depositors. He was found out, tried, and sentenced to a stiff prison term. Unrepentant, he told the judge, "Those big city banks can afford to lose money a lot easier than my people back home."

An old Masonic emblem appears (**above*****) on a building in Telluride. Fraternal orders were a powerful force in early mining camps.***
The mountains rise steeply from town (**opposite*****). Like some other mining towns, including Vail and Aspen, Telluride now is a popular ski area.***

UTAH

Mormons and mining rarely mixed. But these brave pioneers also left a heritage of ghost towns as they settled their new homeland.

Old Deseret Pioneer Village

The Mormons, as the members of the Church of Jesus Christ of Latter-Day Saints are called, went West seeking, not gold, but religious freedom. They were the antithesis of the forty-niners: deeply religious, mostly farmers, with a strong sense of family and community. They neither smoked, drank, or cursed. But they outlasted the prospectors, and are a strong influence throughout most of the West today. Not to understand the Mormons and their singular contribution is to have an incomplete picture of the western migration in the last half of the nineteenth century.

This religion was founded in 1830 by Joseph Smith in New York State. He was said to have had visions of God, Jesus Christ, and the Angel Moroni, who showed Smith where gold plates engraved with undiscovered books of the Bible were hidden.

From the beginning, Mormons were subjected to religious prosecution. They moved, first to Ohio, then Missouri, then Illinois where Joseph Smith was shot and killed by a mob. His successor, Brigham Young, led a large wagon train west. In 1847, when the party of 143 men, three women, and two children arrived in the valley of the Great Salt Lake, Brigham Young said, "This is the place" and they settled there. The rest of the Mormons joined them later.

The Mormons flourished in Utah. To farm in the desert, they divided the land into small parcels and built dams, canals, and ditches to provide irrigation. In the Mormons' first growing season, flocks of sea gulls saved their crops by eating great swarms of crickets. To commemorate the event, a statue of sea gulls later was erected in Temple Square in Salt Lake City. Indian problems soon were overcome as the Mormons followed Brigham Young's advice that it was cheaper to feed them than to fight them.

The Mormons organized the State of Deseret. (In the Book of Mormon, deseret is the word for honeybee, the symbol of industry.) Brigham Young was the governor and spiritual leader. The state applied for admission to the Union, but was refused. The Territory of Utah was created instead in 1840. The biggest obstacle to statehood was the Mormon practice of polygamy. The antipathy between the Mormons and the federal government died out after the abolishment of polygamy, and Utah was admitted as the 45th state in 1896.

At the entrance to Emigrant Canyon in Salt Lake City, where Mormon pioneers first entered the valley, is the Old Deseret Pioneer Village. This collection of vintage buildings includes Brigham Young's Forest Farm Home, and it is a living testimonial to the faith and industry of an outstanding group of pioneers.

A monument to Brigham Young (*above*) stands at the spot where he first saw the valley of the Great Salt Lake.
A sturdy social hall (*opposite*) is part of Old Deseret.

*A steer (***above***) takes his leisure near a barn in Old Deseret. The village is a living museum, portraying pioneer living as it developed from temporary dugouts to the comparative comforts of substantial adobe houses (***below***). Nearby are sections of the final thirty-five miles of the Mormon Trail.*

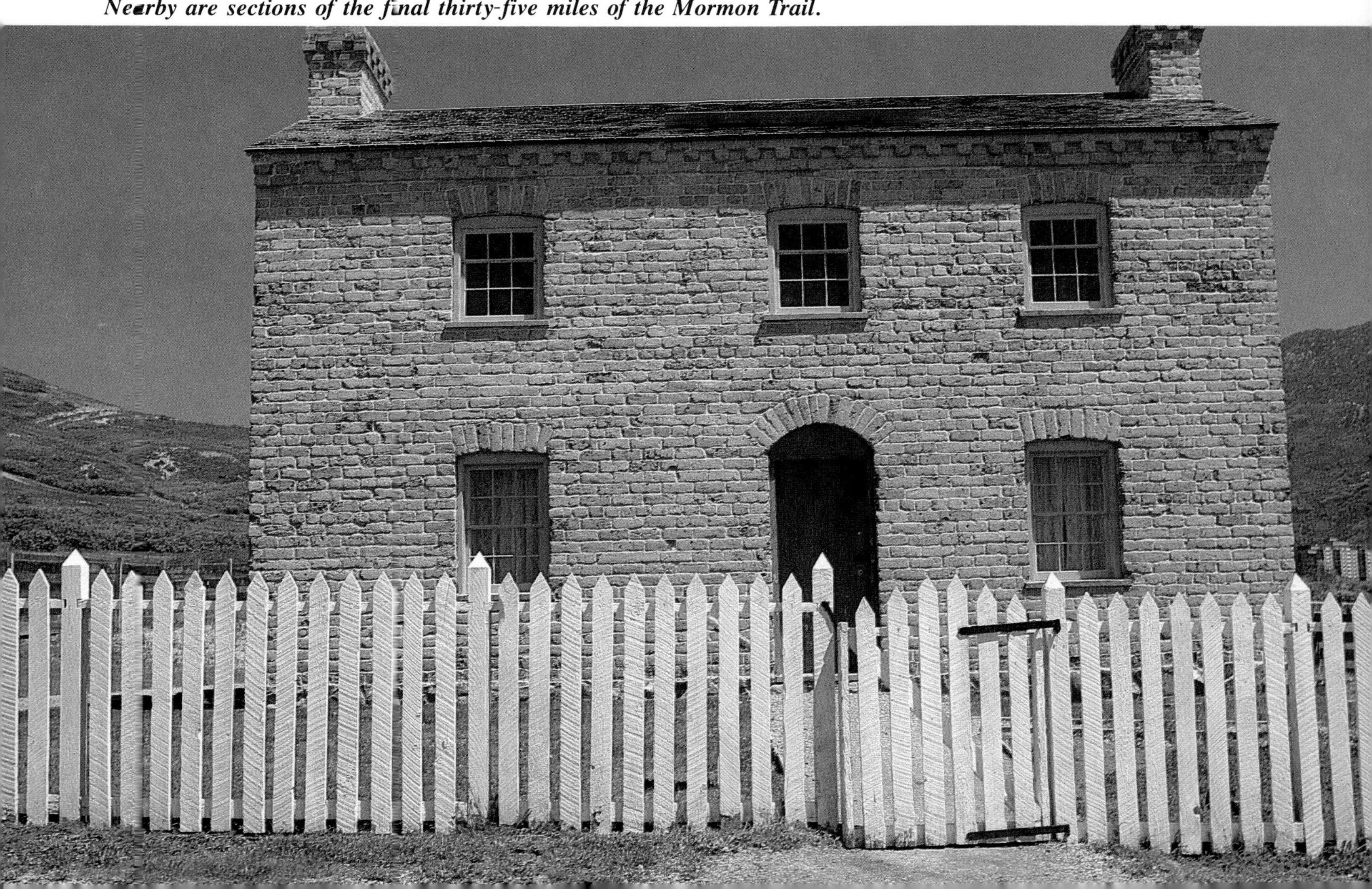

This stucco and frame house (above) is representative of more recent pioneer homes. Unlike the slapdash construction in mining camps, the Mormons built even their barns to last (below). The village concentrates on the period from the original settlement in 1847, to 1869 when the railroad came.

Salt Lake City

Salt Lake City is hardly a ghost town. To the contrary, it is one of the most beautiful and progressive cities in the country, superbly situated seventeen miles from the Great Salt Lake, with great mountains rising to the east and west. It is one of the most carefully planned cities: Temple Square is the center and the streets were laid out in grid fashion, streets that are 132 feet wide and lined with trees.

It is hard to imagine that Salt Lake City today isn't pretty much what Brigham Young had in mind. The town that the early Mormon pioneers wrested from the barren desert has grown sensibly and gracefully into an industrious, businesslike city that somehow retains the warmth and charm of a much smaller community.

Of particular interest to the visitor are the three buildings at Temple Square: the Tabernacle, the Temple, and the Assembly Hall. It is hard to conceive that three buildings of such beauty and sophistication were built in the American West in a period when early Victorian was in vogue.

Temple Square, and the city around it, are evidence of the invincibility of the human spirit.

***The Assembly Hall* (above) *is classic counterpoint to the majestic Mormon Temple* (opposite).**

BELLE STARR
RESTAURANT
THE
WAY
STATION

Heber Springs City

This is the home of the famous Heber Creeper, an antique train that takes passengers on a three-and-a-half hour ride through some of the most spectacular scenery in the West. It winds down through Heber Valley and Provo Canyon to Bridal Veil Falls, dropping several thousand feet as it goes.

Around the station is Heber Pioneer Village, a charming collection of old-time buildings that capture the feel of Utah a century ago. In the background rise the Washatch Mountains, including Mt. Timpanogos—one of the most impressive in the state. Each building in the village has something to see, do, or buy that is suggestive of the early days.

The area around Heber City is ranch country and livestock is shipped to market from here. Four miles away in the mountains are crater mineral springs called hot pots. There are excellent trout streams nearby, and the area is known for its hunting.

The sense of community is so much a part of the Mormon ethic that it has given an unusual quality to its rural areas. Whenever possible, farmers and ranchers live in town and villages, commuting to their acreage.

Riding the Heber Creeper and wandering around the village, one is reminded of what Wallace Stegner once wrote: "Say that the West is everybody's romantic home, for we have all spent a part of our childhood here."

Water cascades down the two levels of Bridal Falls (above). The best way to enjoy this memorable sight is to ride here on the Heber Creeper.
The Wasatch Mountains form a dramatic background to the Pioneer Village (opposite) which is the home of the antique train known as the Heber Creeper. On summer weekends, there are trains that serve dinner to passengers.

GREG
n
HELEN
Devon

Spring Canyon

There was gold and silver to be found in Utah, but the early Mormons were discouraged from mining, except for their own needs. "We cannot eat gold and silver," counseled Brigham Young. For most of the last half of the nineteenth century, prospectors considered Utah simply a place to travel through on their way to California and Nevada diggings.

One minable substance the Mormons could use, though, was coal—and it was found in abundance in several locations—including Spring Canyon, near Helper, some one hundred miles southeast of Provo. In the 1890's a number of coal mining towns developed in Spring Canyon, among them Peerless, Spring Canyon, Standardville, Rains, and Mutual. They flourished for about a quarter of a century, then were abandoned as the coal gave out. Today all are ghost towns and it is almost impossible to tell where one town ended and another began.

On either side of the narrow winding road up into the canyon are the remains of houses, mines, schools, stores, and other buildings. Here and there are small stretches of railroad track, all that's left of a spur line to the mines. The scars of mining are healing, and the canyon once again is becoming a place of tranquil beauty. There are signs that a few families are moving into Spring Canyon to live, but not to mine.

The remains of a miner's house* (above) *peek down from the side of Spring Canyon.

Graffiti decorates the crumbling walls of a mine building* (opposite). *The introduction of natural gas for home heating was one of the factors that led to the closing of many of the state's coal mines.

A mine building of corrugated tin (above) is falling prey to the elements. The remainder of one mine (below) sprawls down the side of Spring Canyon. In 1900 at Scofield, about ten miles from Spring Canyon, but not reachable through the canyon, occurred one of the worst mining disasters in American history.

Railroad ties and tracks (**above**) *are all that's left of the spur line that once transported coal from the mines to the railhead at Helper. Tumbledown mine buildings* (**below**) *often are looted by people seeking weathered wood, popular in some decorating. Snakes are also attracted to such ruins.*

Grafton

In 1861, Brigham Young announced to his followers that he was sending Mormons from the Salt Lake City area to settle in Dixie, as southern Utah was then called. They were to grow cotton, have children, and start a town.

The town of Grafton was settled just south of the mountains that now form Zion National Park. Cotton was planted, about one acre for each of the town's twenty-eight families. Flocks of sheep were used to produce wool, from which the settlers made their own clothing. Some families experimented with mulberry trees as a source of food. Mulberries are similar to blackberries, except they fall off the tree when ripe.

With Brigham Young's blessing, silk worms were imported, and for awhile the area successfully produced good quality silk. Grafton, however, didn't fare as well as its neighbors. It was plagued with spring floods and Indian raids. The headstones in the small cemetery here attest to the number of residents slain by Indians. At one point during the Indian troubles, Grafton was abandoned. The people returned when a peace treaty was signed, but Grafton never really became the community all hoped it would be. Population dwindled in the early part of this century, and by 1921 Grafton was too small to be recognized as a unit of the Mormon Church.

Only two or three families were living in Grafton in 1950 when it served as the setting for a Disney movie. Now it is a true ghost town—with a difference. The quality of construction of the buildings, and the neatness with which the town was laid out are unmistakably Mormon. Fate was to prove otherwise, but Grafton was built to last.

The doors are gone from this Grafton house, (*above*) and the solidly constructed walls are beginning to list.
The red brick schoolhouse (*opposite*) has withstood the years rather well. Inside, an English lesson still remains written neatly on the blackboard.

*A neat log cabin (**above**) is starting to crumble, and the roof on another building (**below**) is following suit. The majestic mountains behind Grafton (**opposite**) now are part of Zion National Park. Spring runoffs from these mountains annually flooded Grafton and hindered its development.*

NEVADA

Bound for California, the forty-niners hurried past mountains which a decade later would start to yield incredible fortunes in silver.

Rhyolite

As Tonopah and Goldfield boomed, prospectors flocked to the surrounding area, and in 1904, Frank "Shorty" Harris and Eddie Cross found promising ore on the way to the Keane Wonder Mine in Death Valley. They named their mine the Bullfrog because of the green color of the ore. Hundreds of miners arrived into the area and a promoter laid out the town of Rhyolite. The cry was "Bullfrog or Bust!"

By the summer of 1905, Rhyolite had a newspaper and a post office. Financier Charles Schwab bought a mine here and built a large mill. Promoters were pushing stock schemes to bankroll mining operations. Property values were rising, credit was plentiful, and soon telephone and telegraph lines, and the Las Vegas and Tonopah Railroad, came to town. By 1907 the population had reached six thousand. The town had four banks, a $20,000 school, four newspapers, a red light district, a casino, numerous saloons, and an air of total confidence.

The financial panic of 1907 ended all that. Smaller mines closed, and the larger mines sharply cut back production. Investment money and credit dried up. By 1910, Rhyolite had only 675 people; by 1920, one. Only a few buildings still stand in Rhyolite now.

The town was built with every confidence in the future, (above) but the financial panic of 1907 ended the dream in the desert.
Weeds now grow in what once were busy streets (opposite). Four newspapers and two magazines once served Rhyolite citizens.

This stately relic (**opposite**) *once was once of Rhyolite's four banks. In the boom years many came to town in cars. One never made it out* (**above**). *Weathering luggage waits on a baggage cart* (**below**) *at the depot for trains that will never come. Millions of dollars in ore once came from nearby mines.*

Tonopah

"Big Jim" Butler was a rancher who spent all his free time prospecting. He was traveling through the desert in the spring of 1900, and decided to stop for the night at an old Indian camp called Tonopah—the Shoshone word for a small desert shrub. In the morning, one of his burros strayed. Butler found it behind a ledge on Mount Oddie, taking shelter from the wind. He took some samples from the ledge, while waiting for the wind to die down.

Some prospectors back in Belmont looked at Butler's samples and told him they were worthless. He threw them away, but later went back to Mount Oddie for more. He took these to his friend, Tasker Oddie, a young lawyer from the East. "I'm broke," he told Oddie, "but you get this assayed and I'll give you a quarter of my claims." It seemed that Oddie was broke as well, but he traded half of his quarter in return for an ordinary eight-dollar assay. The analysis showed a potential yield of 640 ounces of silver, and $206 in gold per ton of ore!

Butler started a number of mines: the Burro, the Desert Queen, Valley View, Silver Top, and Buckboard. He asked his wife to pick out a mining spot and name it. She did, and dubbed it the Mizpah, which proved to be the richest on record. Butler also leased mining areas for 25 percent of the gross.

A town quickly sprang up. Wells were dug and an ice plant built. In two years there were thirty saloons, but Tonopah was surprisingly peaceful, perhaps because Wyatt Earp had been appointed marshal.

Philadelphia interests bought into the mines and expanded the operation. By 1906 the mines were producing $10 million annually.

The good years lasted until the mid 1920's, then Tonopah slowly petered out. There was a lot of excitement in 1969 when Howard Hughes bought up more than a hundred of the original claims, but after some assays were run, nothing happened. Tonopah settled back into its long sleep in the desert.

The Mizpah Hotel* (above) *was named after the richest mine discovered at Tonopah. The bar and restaurant in the hotel displays memorabilia of Jack Dempsey, who once was the bouncer in a local saloon. The deserted mine building* (opposite) *stands watch over Tonopah.

The barren hills around Tonopah yielded up a fortune in silver from 1900 until the start of World War II. Now the shafts and mine buildings look down on the community that has dwindled from some thirty thousand people, to less than two thousand.

Goldfield

An Indian named Tom Fisherman found some gold ore at Columbia Mountain, and brought it to the silver mining camp at Tonopah, thirty miles to the north. The ore was not very rich, but it caught the attention of two young miners, Billy Marsh and Harry Stimler. They got a grubstake and headed south on a buckboard, drawn by a mule and a horse.

They made camp at the base of Malapai Mesa, and within a few weeks struck gold on the side of Columbia Mountain. By the spring of 1903 a tent camp had risen, first named Grandpa, (in hopes it would be the grandpa of all the mining camps) then Goldfield. The strikes at Goldfield kept getting richer and richer, and by 1904 it was a community of eight thousand. A railroad linking Goldfield to Tonopah was built in 1905.

To spur the growth of the town, local saloon owner "Tex" Rickard

The arch* (above) *hasn't fallen, but practically everything around it has. It's hard to look at what's left of Goldfield today* (opposite) *and imagine it as a booming town with its own stock exchange, four banks, and luxurious hotels and restaurants.

promoted the Joe Gans-Battling Nelson lightweight championship fight with a $30,000 purse, displayed in $20 gold pieces in the window of the bank. More than fifteen thousand fans saw the fight on Labor Day, 1906. It went forty-two rounds, Gans winning on a foul. Rickard had found his calling, and went on to be one of the greatest fight promoters of all time, and the principal architect of Jack Dempsey's career.

Goldfield continued to thrive, despite the depression of 1907 and a bitter miners' strike that finally necessitated the intervention of federal troops to restore order.

The peak year was 1910, when the mines produced more than $11 million in bullion.

Goldfield declined slowly. A flash flood in 1913 did considerable damage, a fire ten years later, considerably more. The big mines shut down in 1919.

Was this house (**above**) *a victim of the 1923 fire, or did it simply die of old age? It's impossible to tell. Two shacks* (**below**) *on the edge of town have seen a lot of history. The saloon* (**opposite**) *is still in operation, and claims to be* **the** *drinking establishment in the state.*

SALOON
The Original Santa Fé Club · Est. 1905
FOOTHILL BLVD.
NO DOGS ALLOWED

Belmont

Throughout the West, difficulties between miners, owners, and the union were common—and all too often flared into violence. Miners worked long and hard, in dangerous conditions, for little pay. The owners thought the miners were stealing from them, which they often did. And the unions were as welcome to the owners as a nest of rattlesnakes.

Most mining camps have ugly incidents in their past. Two union organizers came to this central Nevada mining town in the 1870s, and were run off. They stopped for the night in a mine tunnel near town, where they were found the next morning. They were taken back to Belmont and hanged on the main street. One was a boy of fifteen.

Belmont's boom only lasted about twenty years, during which time its mines produced $15 million in silver and lead, before petering out in 1885. Several attempts to resume operations came to naught. Turquoise was discovered in 1909, but the deposits weren't extensive enough to be profitable. A flotation mill was built in 1914, but after a few years of operation, closed down. A 1921 stamp mill was equally unsuccessful.

Several interesting buildings remain in Belmont. One is the Cosmopolitan Music Hall. Once star performers entertained crowds of miners here. Another relic is the old courthouse, built in 1867 when Belmont was the seat of Nye County. Today there are a few houses, a crumbling wall here and there, some mine buildings, and little else.

Tinwork on the dome of the schoolhouse* (above) *still gleams in the afternoon sun. The corpse of the Cosmopolitan Music Hall* (opposite) *which was once painted bright red and green. Now, the sun streams through holes in the roof.

*The roof of the Nye County Courthouse can be seen through the wall of an old store (***above***). Part of Belmont's main street (***below***) is losing its battle with time and weeds. From 1865 to 1885, some $15 million in silver and lead came from the mine here. Now, all that's left is the pile of smelter.*

Goldpoint

Some ghost towns are rich in history; some, like Goldpoint, are not. There was a strike, of course, but much of the value of the ore was lost in the poor mining processes used in the early days. The town changed its name from Hornsilver to Goldpoint in 1929 to spruce up its image, but the change didn't seem to do much good. A number of law suits concerning the mill finally killed the town.

Goldpoint, however, is representative of so many ghost towns in Nevada and deserves more than a passing glance. Goldpoint is in the barren wastes of western Nevada, less than 250 miles from the towns of the California Mother Lode country, but the contrast couldn't be sharper. The Mother Lode country is beautiful with grassy, rolling hills, trees, rivers, and lakes. The climate is temperate, the rainfall ample. Gold or no, it is a nice place to live.

Most of Nevada—known as Western Utah in the early mining days—is flat, hard land where little grows but mesquite, Joshua trees, and cactus. The summers are long and cruelly hot, the winters short and cold. Water always is a problem. The average rainfall is less than ten inches, and practically all of that falls in the winter. Rivers trickle through the area most of the year, and flood in the spring.

When the mining days were over in California, a great number of the people stayed on, turning to ranching or farming to support themselves. But when the mines played out in Nevada, there was nothing the miners could turn to. It was move on or perish.

Few ghost towns are as lonely as those in Nevada.

The headframe of the mine rises above the general store in Goldpoint* (above)*. The headstone of an early miner* (opposite) *stands in Goldpoint's tiny cemetery.

GEORGE. WA
GIBSON. Bor
S. CAROLIN
18
Died AUG

A miner's tools mounted over the door of this old shack, (above) *apparently weren't sufficient to bring luck to the miner who lived here. Gas was a bargain* (above) *when Goldpoint was breathing its last gasps in the early 1950's.*

With miles upon miles of open land, it seems strange that miners' shacks were so close together (above), but the desert wasn't conducive to growing lawns. Goldpoint's post office didn't make it to the age of zip codes.

HARDWARE
1869
RED GARTER
KENO
FREE
WYATT EARP'S FARO TABLE
COMSTOCK GOLD SCALES
1905 FIRE
CANADIAN AT PAR

Virginia City

The early days of the bonanza at Virginia City read like a medieval morality play, except, perhaps, for the absence of a figure to represent morality. The seven deadly sins were very much in evidence.

Silver had been discovered in Virginia City in 1850, but the prospectors were bound for California and gold. It wasn't until 1859 that Peter O'Riley and Pat McLaughlin struck a rich vein on Mt. Davidson. As they were working their claim, along came a fast-talking con man named Henry Comstock. After accusing them of claim jumping, Comstock allowed himself to become a partner in return for forgetting about his bogus claim. Comstock cajoled and blustered his way into a piece of so many claims in the area, that it became known as the Comstock Lode.

Time has not run out for Virginia City* (above)*. The 600 or so residents often greet as many as 40,000 tourists a summer weekend. One of the major attractions is the action along C Street* (opposite)*. Virginia City is the most visited "ghost town" in the country.

The Bonanza days left a rich legacy of Victoriania. St. Mary's in the Mountains (opposite) *has a large bell cast from Comstock silver. The Fourth Ward School* (above) *and the Cole Mansion* (below) *are masterpieces of Victorian architecture. All three buildings were erected after the 1875 fire.*

An amiable drunk named James Finney and his partners struck a rich deposit at what was to become Gold Hill. Finney, known as Old Virginny, is credited with naming the town after his native state. But the early winners of Gold Hill came to unfortunate ends. Comstock sold out for $11,000, and committed suicide a few years later. Peter O'Riley sold out, and ended up in an insane asylum. Pat McLaughlin became a ranch cook, before finding a pauper's grave. Finney sold his share for a bottle of whiskey and a blind horse. The one who benefited from the miners' misfortune was George Hearst. The Hearst family fortune, expanded by his son William Randolph Hearst, had its beginnings in the Ophir.

Clever stock manipulation and incredible luck made four men—James Fair, James Flood, John Mackay and William S. O'Brien—"Kings of the Comstock." They secretly bought up stock in the area of their holdings at distress prices, before announcing their bonanza. This ploy netted the four men an estimated $160 million.

Other fortunes were made in Virginia City. William Sharon, who arrived in 1864, loaned money to miners and mill owners, and took over their property when a recession came. Adolph Sutro parlayed his scheme of building tunnels to drain and ventilate the mines into millions. Others became rich backing the Virginia and Truckee Railroad.

Virginia City was the richest city of its size in the world, and it lived up to its reputation. There were mansions and an opera house. A luxury hotel in Virginia City had the only elevator between Chicago and San Francisco. By the middle 1870's, Virginia City had a population of more than 30,000 people. No one saw a cloud on the horizon, but there was an end to even this mountain of silver.

But what years they were! The best estimates say that from 1859 to the end of the century, the Comstock Lode yielded one billion dollars in silver and gold.

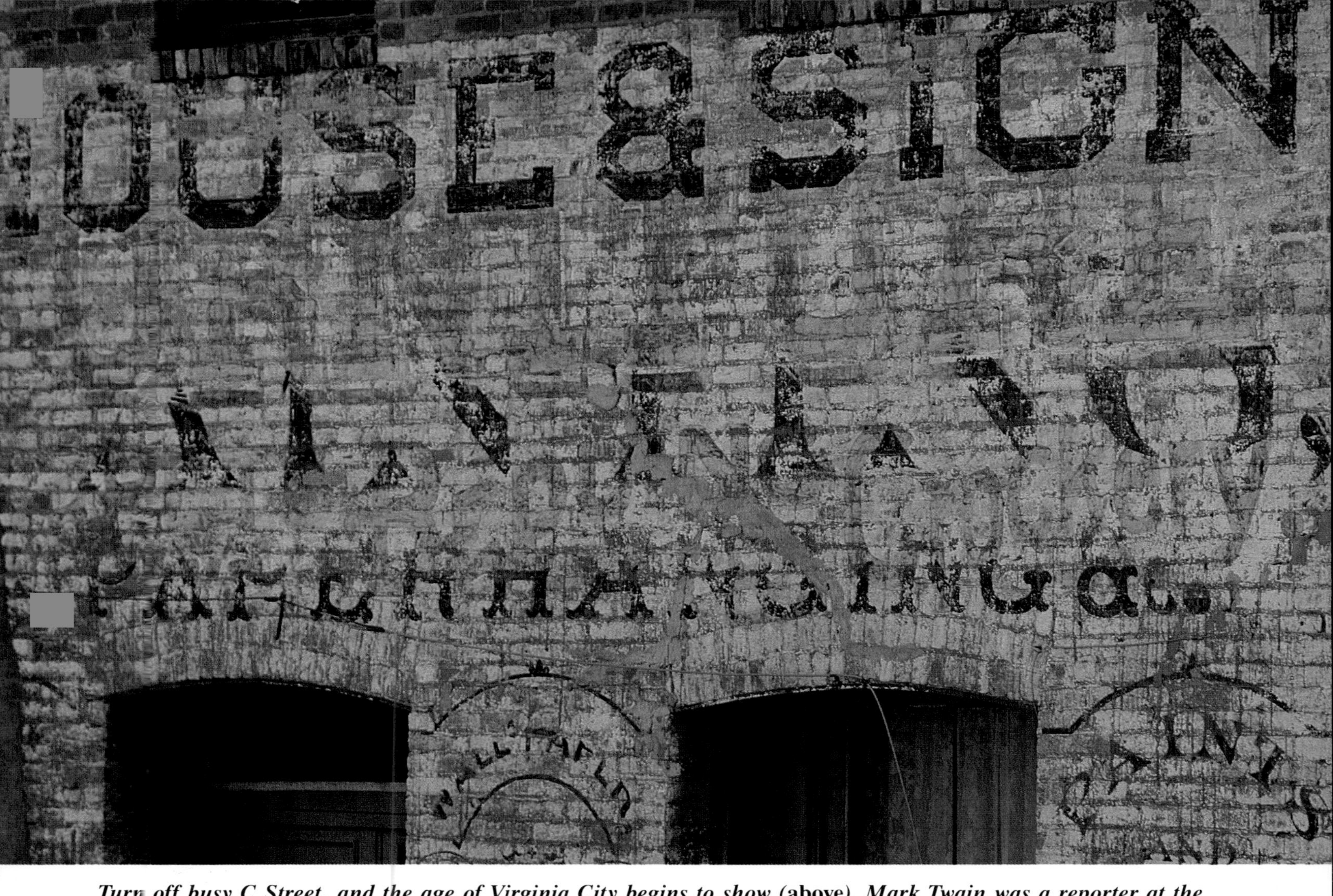

Turn off busy C Street, and the age of Virginia City begins to show (above). *Mark Twain was a reporter at the* Territorial Enterprise (below) *after trying his hand at mining. There is a small Twain museum in the building, and much of the original press equipment and furniture has been retained.*

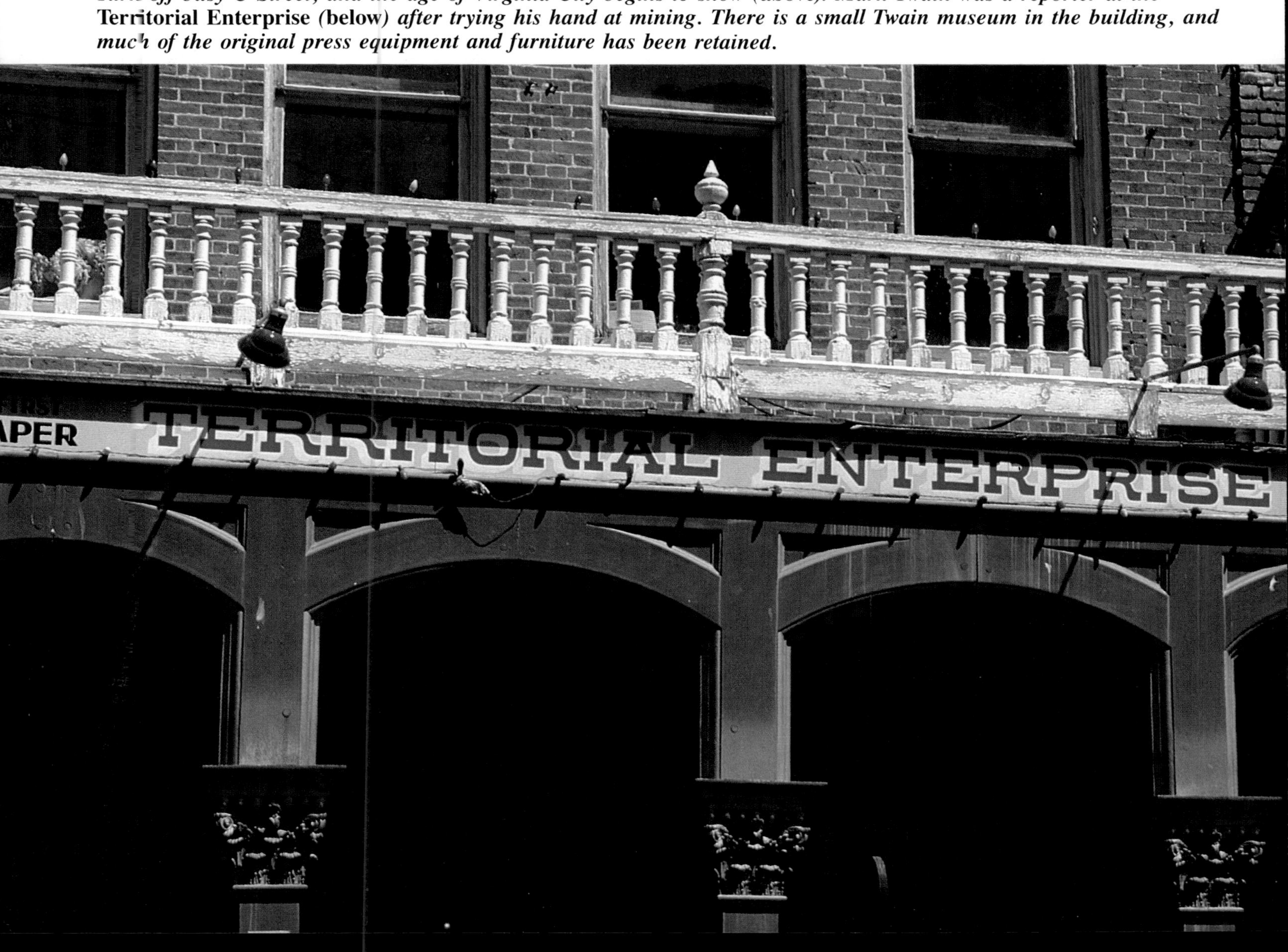

*Financial institutions such as the Nevada Bank (*above*) were kept hopping during the bonanza. The song* **The Face on the Bar Room Floor** *supposedly was inspired by Virginia City, possibly by this painting. Saloons and gambling houses still are here in abundance, and are popular with Virginia City visitors.*

The Bowers Mansion

Sandy Bowers had been a Missouri mule skinner, a man described by his friends as "an honest, kindhearted soul, born and reared in the lower ranks, and miraculously ignorant." Scottish-born Eilley Orrum had married a Mormon in the Washoe Valley, but when the Mormons were called back to Salt Lake City, she stayed on and opened a boardinghouse. Sandy Bowers was one of her boarders.

Sandy owned a claim on a ten-foot strip of mining property. Eilley owned the one next to it; she had taken it over from a miner who couldn't pay for his room and board. The bonanza came and they found their claims were netting $18,000 a month. They decided to marry. Before long their claims were paying $100,000 a month.

Eilley had dreamed of a home and children. She had given birth to two children by her first husband, but they had died in infancy. Eilley decided she would have the most beautiful home in Washoe Valley, a $200,000 granite mansion with a commanding view of the valley.

To furnish their new home, the Bowers sailed for Europe. They commissioned custom-made furniture in Italy, specially designed and woven carpets, silver sets, moroccan-bound books. They returned to Nevada 18 months later, planning a gala housewarming, but it wasn't to be The new society leaders of Virginia City chose to snub the Bowers and their mansion.

It was the beginning of hard times. The mine was becoming exhausted; new machinery had to be purchased. Soon after the machinery was installed, a spring flooded the mine with mud and slime. Working all night, Sandy caught a cold that was to prove fatal.

The Bowers' estate was valued at $638,000, but that was an illusion. Sandy had sold too much stock to retain control of the mine. His investments had proved worthless. Creditors pressed claims against the estate.

*Romantic Victorian statuary (***opposite, above***) graces the living room in the mansion. Built of granite, the mansion (***above***) was the best money could buy in the early 1900s. The Bowers made an extended European trip to purchase furnishings for their new home. The furniture for the bedrooms (* **below***) was handcrafted in Italy.*